THE
MALAY
OUTCAST

THE
MALAY
OUTCAST

Due to their,
- Non Leadership
- Too much amusement
- Shallow in thinking
- & Non religiously

ZULKEFLI PUTEH

PARTRIDGE

This is my 'self-publishing'. I solely work on this then the only know.
Any question, discussion, complaint should be direct to me and nothing with the publisher or any other third party/ies.
Zulkefli Puteh
May 2016

Print information available on the last page.

To order additional copies of this book, contact
Toll Free 800 101 2657 (Singapore)
Toll Free 1 800 81 7340 (Malaysia)
orders.singapore@partridgepublishing.com

www.partridgepublishing.com/singapore

Contents

Dedication

This is my dedication to;

1) My former boss (employer) Johari Saleh of Winpower Corporation from whom I had very big opportunity to explore, learn and handling various type (field) of highly technical equipment.
2) My country and to every individual honest and loyal citizen.

Biography

The author is Kedahan (Northern State of Malaysia), born on December 25th, the Christmas day of 1956.

He was Malay entrepreneur who was fail in his engineering entrepreneurship in Klang Valley. His effort only can sustain until 1998 just for 14 years of period.

Then he became free-lance specialist on scientific and high tech equipment/instruments.

His job was inclusively repair, service, modification, planning and installation (especially new equipment), shifting and refurbishment mainly didactic for universities, colleges and polytechnics.

It is also including design of small machines, iron structures (building, trusses), framework and system (like conveyor or elevator) for contractors, factories, institutions (like standard body-i.e. SIRIM in Malaysia).

Beside that he also involve in shipbuilding and maintenance plus certain special projects.

He started his primary school in Kedah, SK Siputeh, then secondary SM Pulau Nyiur and SM Sultan Abdul Halim, Jitra.

Then he joins UKM (National University of Malaysia) as one of the pioneer students of matriculation course and become student after.

He fails to finish his study in UKM.

Alternatively, later he obtains his Diploma in Mechanical Engineering from Bedford College of Kuala Lumpur and Certificate in Electrical and Instrumentation from Chemical Company of Malaysia Bhd (ICI group of companies).

In UKM he strives to get substantial knowledge in physics and chemistry which it is then real applied along his carrier.

With his low intellectuality and low IQ he cannot carry the 'truck load' of so many subjects in one go which is not related to the core subject. (There is about time where the syllabus starts pushing to compact doubling and doubling and variety).

He walks out in third year with a lot of useful (for his life) and tangible knowledge without any degree is very thankful to UKM.

About the Author

The Failure and free-lance job was gave him tremendously a lot of experience (in variety) with in huge range of works, for example:

o   Precision and rough[1]
o   Hygienic *(food & drugs)* and sewage *(machinery and pumps)*;
o   Bull power and brain power;
o   Underground and tower;
o   Tableland and high hill;
o   Shipbuilding and anchorage (International water);
o   Welding/climbing and paper work;
o   Design and fabricate *(machine and iron works)*;
o   Installation and refurbishment;
o   Blue jacket and neck-tie *(white collar)*;
o   Decent car and lorry (small);
o   Low class and high class (+ expatriate);
o   Train/Teach/instruct the people and attend technical course/seminar;
o   Malaysia and over sea;
o   Coffee shop/food stall and coffee house;
o   Small enterprise and Public Listed companies.
o   Tender and auction;
o   Police station, IPD (district) and IPK (contingent);
o   Beggars and gangsters;
o   Cleaver and pistol;
o   Court and prison.

---

[1]   Like milligram weighing scale and laser measurement device and tonnage weighing scale for lorry and railway coach

As his faith (in Muslim) he keens to admonish anybody (except sultans) preferably in writing (more responsibility) with his own signature. May be this is drive for emerges of this book. Some earlier experiences were in:

- 1984-Goodyear Tire (American director) - a few series and total more than 100 pages.
- 1990-ITM (Mara Institute of Technology, now university); it is about 20 pages.
- 1999-Islamic courts judges (Selangor) – series of 4 booklets for the total about 400 pages; (gradually some bombastic)
- 2005-KUKUM's (now UniMap, University Malaysia Perlis) reactor – 4 series of email for the total of 16 pages;
- 2006-2007- the 5th Prime Minister Abdullah Badawi – series of 5 booklets (Warkah untuk Pak Lah), total of 1,000 pages; (gradually then bombastic)
- 2008-2009 – DPM, then PM Datuk Seri Najib Abdul Razak – series of 3 booklets, total of 121 pages.

He is very hateful and regret when seeing any hypocrite leader who is talking nonsense, claim flourish success but in actual is upside down. He prefers any leader to keep quiet or at least don't talk contrary.

This book refers to his real face to face public experience and also his own experience in difficulty and hardship time. As his experience he used to eat rice 2 or 3 days once (following by biscuits on next a few day alternately) with 2 or 3 packets of noodles with heavy liquidate for his family of five.

He never regret as he can help to voice out in real ground of poverty which most of them just only can cry nobody want to listen to them.

With no choice (in thinking of his believe and for his life in the Day After) he has to become non salary 'representative' for people.

In this book he continues his admonition to the leader with some offer of his old alternative (earlier) proposals (if they don't have) since 2007.

Any leader should avoid from too much depend on old fashion thinking, classical 'vertical logic' sometimes should change to 'horizontal imagination' – lateral thinking. If one still maintains 'vertical logic'; 'the iron cannot fly' but now everybody know differently, 600 tonnes can fly with 6 engines.

His principle is universal; the leader (who claim as Muslim) must be clever enough for whole citizen and definitely not for his own and crony (like Saidina Umar, who always become last and so on).

Any leader who is reaching the point of 'no more capable', no gut to benefit for people has to step down peacefully like most gentleman non-Muslim leader does.

The country no needs to be ruin for the sake of any leader.

He strong believe the God (Allah on his faith) has put him in details of every step by step since beginning for all of this to be happen because it is was proven that he is not clever man and with low IQ.

Prologue

I am very sorry to my English and whatever related to this book.

This is self-publishing. So nobody outside should bear the responsibility. Everything should be direct to me.

This is special case 'not a book' just 'a grumble from the sky' and assimilate in the book shape and incomparable.

I just supposed to write in Malay but then due to the 'standard' Malay problem all the way, inadvertently I found this way out.

Finally you can see this bad and maybe the ugliest book. I'm realised but I had no effort to transfer this book into proper manner. So, please don't consider this is a proper book to refer except for the point of idea.

Coffee shop

This is a coffee shop (not coffee house) and itinerant food stall standard of discussion. The traditional English syntax sometime not make a sense or it will tend to be wrong meaning or meaningless to the current and local context.

Bombastic! Yes the sound is due to too long way to wait *rakyats'* (citizen) acceptable result. Very long stories, program with poetic, flamboyant, shouting, crying, censure (whoever with dissenting opinion) bragging and whatever projection still need proper deadline.

Tomorrow *rakyats'* bread and butter or children's school fees cannot wait to another Malaysia general election to receive windfall from swarm of Malay government bees. They no need a billion or a million even hundreds of thousand dollars. They count dollar and cent and tightly grasp securely even just a coin. It must be clearly understood by any country leader.

Most of peoples especially administrators or leaders are need to be admonishing. In Islamic faith it was stressed a lot in the Quran. This two is common reference (Quran-51Adz Dzaariyaat; 55). (Quran-87Al A'laa; 9).

Even Prophet Mohammed had admonished by the God (Quran-80 Abasa)[2]. It looks like a small matter. Maybe it is purposely small case is to shows how important it is as guidance. Large troop of elephants soldiers sometime least impact to a single mosquito that can kill a greatest king.

Everybody need a good advice / adviser and should listen for whatever would become the 'mandatory' solution.

For example; 'You cannot do anything regarding high tech to the Malays… and sub-example; Sabirin[3] with 100 engineers make small satellite maybe about a quarter size of a car with the cost of RM400 million within 3 or 4 years

Typical Malay who with 'Menberuk'[4] brainchild will think it was a rubbish drum because it looks alike. Yeah 400 million rubbish drum as about the cost of making Proton (Malaysia national car) plant in 1980's or half price of Penang Bridge.

Since environmentally is good, the choice is back to agriculture but it should be in new 'synergy'. Mechanise, gradually adopt some technology and move to more on machine-assisted rather than labour intensive, concentrate more on small-holders, you will be reward with very clear way out.

Then Malay majority will have a lot of thing to do. No more free time for stupid politicking like their Malay leaders who is twenty four hours per day and 365 days a year until next general election. Off that time if any just for plundering whatever could and for distributing loot amongst their gang.

Bombastic

SPECIAL NOTE: By some sincerely advice, this book was reviewed due to the 'bombastic'. Right now the readers should be in mild taste.

Maybe question arouse, why should be bombastic. The answer is too much time waiting and promise for significant effect but now worse and very crucial even for basic need. The Malay leader just simply ignores and consequences all the time badly spend out for real poverty.

No more delay is acceptable, either outcast or go back to start all over again. At the moment the 'time' is already sharper than a sword to outcast the Malaysian

---

[2]   He tries to facing off from the blind poor guy who had requested for advice, focus on nobleman.
[3]   News BH16/03/09 – ATSB, Astronautic. Please see in Chapter 3; 7.1 - Sabirin
[4]   'Menberuk' – Scrap Iron Mentality, ref. Part 6.3.

Malay but the Malay leader as usual will sing his demented song "Malaysian ♫♫on track♪ towards high♫ income status♩♪$$$$.......".

Hopefully this will support the entire movement of Malaysian salvage. "Inchal ♫lahhh♩♪….. God willing.….♩♪…..", sang of Salvatore Adamo.

If you still need to talk about soft and polite admonishing, we can jump to part 5 – The Current Situation. Then we quote an example newspaper cutting -'Global Competitiveness'[5] Or very much earlier (Nov 2008), with very politeness of Anuar Mohd Nor who is UMNO (United Malays National Organisation) backbencher itself already express out the worry which become true right now in his magazine 'Suara Baru'[6]. This was distributing until Brunei.

The Malay leader won't cares and makes like nothing to be happen to the Malay. The Malay is just lean on the rotten railing of vessel deck and 24 hours fighting. Fight and fight to be outcast as the main major job.

Now we can continue all these matter in there (Part 5).

Coffee House

Another area of concern is why not 'coffee house'.

It was needed accordingly. This book exists not for the sake of making the book but 'crying of hardship, poignant and non-heard voice of *rakyat* (citizen)'. The target is for all level of society especially middle and lower class.

That you can see a lot of photographs (images) inside. It is the easiest way to everybody, images and imagines – with the images, you no more need to suffer to imagine. There is sometime a complete whole exercise of the book is incomparable to a single of presentable photograph.

'High class' discussion already flooded in the market either forums / reports, books or journal even newspaper. More over there is *Majlis Profesor Negara* (Professor Council) where all professors automatically are a member. There were 14 clusters and much unlimited idea.

Malaysia is not in main disaster belt or perimeter. Any projection is straight-forward not like other country which more jobs to consider earth-quake or heavy

---

5   Ref to – Part 5.2.1 – Global Competitiveness
6   Ref to – Part 6.6.6 – *'Suara Baru'*

rain and landslide. Another area is, real 'bonus' as Malaysia don't have 4 seasons. So easy the Malay leader cannot do?

It is good to remind to everybody, any gradually up for wrong-doing and bribery practise will end like Marcos & Imelda of Philxxxxx. Sooner or later the leader will be pulling down. The longer they 'fight with *rakyat*' (for their own sake) more suffer they will get latter.

'Outside in'

Malay leaders have right time and very good ground and suppose to learn from Tun Mahathir, he 'fight with outside' to flourish domestic economy. Some leaders fight with their own *'rakyat'* to plunder them for absolute poverty. Until now he (Mahathir) never worries to stay in the country and still can be impudent to anybody who deserves it.

So with Lim Kheng Yaik[7] (former minister), "We (Chinese) want to bring 'outside in', don't waste time to quarrel with what we have. 30% you can take. It was agreed. No problem at all. Malay entrepreneurs should thing wisely and not greedy. Help each other, look outside to bring in and success"

'Outside' matters more important. The really significant things for an organization happen on the 'outside'. (M.K.Rustomji, 1986, p. 38)

For our info, in 2008 it's how hard Hasina of Bangladesh (the leader with vision) runs her nation on 'looks Mahathir' and 'Bangladesh full digital 2021'. All seven channel are about Mahathir and Malaysia since the children of 3 or 4 years old suddenly shout 'Mahathir!' as the image appear on TV screen. She who can 'smell' the bright future for her country really respect Mahathir, that why 2021 and not 2020 as Mahathir plan for Malaysia, maybe?

Actually they can speed up and left Malaysia behind because a lot of their Malaysia-experience and hard-working workers already back to Bangladesh. Unfortunately the series of big disasters ruin the country infrastructures and we are lucky to gain indirect credit.

As I learnt from my former worker, Md Mintu from Meherpur, he was trapped (that time is 2009) on fourth floor (somewhere in Chittagong) and his hand phone battery exhausted.

After our last conversation, on the following day, I cannot contact him for almost two weeks.

---

7   Lim Kheng Yaik – please see in chapter 3

He briefs me, he was very lucky that time a lot of peoples and buildings were flush out in disaster. Four or five storey building simply disappears become table land. Beside that they had extreme hot and cold to claim death a lot of people.

We just simply imagine how stupid we are, as a Muslim we cannot admire and utilise what the God gift (Mahathir)? Still alive, Mahathir is belong to the country and he still want to work not to sleep or run away to stay abroad. Historically shows that he cooperates with incumbent PM and his wife and appears in so many occasions until he misled with Malaysian future in his hand.

Current PM maybe forget who his father is, Tun Razak (second Malaysia prime minister) in Malay and Malaysian context. Mahathir declared he owe everything to his father. He (Mahathir) works hard and considers success to continue Tun Razak's vision in his chair fourth prime minister for the sake of Malay and nation survival.

Gradually now current PM become something like against his father's vision, Tun Razak. Unbelievable!

How can he (Mahathir) ignore. If Tun Razak still alive, do we think he will keep quite? Definitely he will become current PM first enemy and not Dr Mahathir. His (Tun Razak) patriotism is well known; only current PM had to pretend don't know due to 'ultimate pressure of QC?'

Back to "why not 'coffee house'"; the problem is The Malay leader and their arse-licker[8] not up to that standard and simply ignores all highly brilliant idea of their own technocrats. The reflection of their class of thinking shows it is very low but 'rakyat' to be sentence and right now they are become hot soup. The country is going bankrupt in no time.

Then the Malay leaders need to 'come down' to see them by lowering their standard and local common phrase (broken English) said 'talk cock' to them as this.

Let continue in Part 5 – Current Situation

---

[8]   arse-licker (Britain)/ass-kisser (N.American)/shoe-licker/sycophant

Chapter 1

THE MALAYSIAN MALAY

PART 1.0 - CIVILIZATION

Before we discuss about Malay leadership which strong tendency to make his clan to be outcast let us track back the Malayan culture and history.

Most of them do not know much about their origin. Some may think that they originate from the Javanese or Bugis of Indonesia or from Yemen, the descendant of Arab traders, or some from Thailand especially those from the northern states. They learned from earlier school books that Kedah and Kelantan once accepted Thai custodian as these states lost the war against Thailand. So many south Thai Malays got cross breed with Malaysian northerners.

Those are clear to today's generation. Anything beyond is flimsy. Not many care to look at history beyond as Malays do not know how to appreciate the past. Anyway more information on Malay civilization can be read on the internet.

1.1 - Pre-War Malay Communities

Life wasn't easy in the old days. Nevertheless, people were contented the way they were. During their parents' and grandparent's days, many of them walked barefoot, as they couldn't afford shoes, which were regarded as a luxury. Boys carried stupid, blunt knives to show off their manhood. Some who came from higher-up families would carry a short, curvy dagger to exhibit their royal connections.

Their parents and grandparents had received early education at age sixteen or seventeen. Boys often studied in open classes or under shady trees because there weren't proper schools at that time. The naughty ones had to be tied to tree trunks to avoid truancy.

1

In spite of being gagged to the teeth, the fathers found their boys floating like ducks, together with the tree trunks, in the nearby river.

Parents went to adult classes to learn to read, like in Run Run Shaws's film *Pendekar Bujang Lapok.*

Boys usually assisted their parents in the paddies or tapping rubber in their village. There weren't serious challenges at that time. Boys played truant, stealing durian, chicken, or eggs for foul play, while the Chinese toiled over small vegetables on small plots or were petty fishmongers. The cranky ones even worked as 'gold miners' (human waste collectors).

People were brought up along racial lines. Malays were dominant masters; the Chinese and Indians were secondary citizens.

That was how the situation was. Life was hard compared with today. Nevertheless, it was they who brought freedom to their land under the banner of unity. The slogan unity we behold and disunity we crumble' was a secret statement that rocked the nation.

Malays generally are peace-loving people. They respect the elderly and vice versa. They have high regard for the elites and the royals. They are patient, faithful, and law-abiding. Nevertheless, they are sleeping tigers if provoked. History has long recorded fighters like Datok Bahaman, Tok Janggut, Tok Kenali, and Lieutenant Adnan, who fought the British, the Japanese, and the communists. It was the Malays' uprising that caused the demise of British resident J W W Birch.

1.2 - Malaya-British Colonialism

The British first set foot in Penang in 1786 and then in Singapore in 1819; they later established the straits settlement in 1830. There wasn't full-scale war resisting the British, not forgetting the Portuguese Alfonso de Albuquerque, who captured Malacca in 1511, and follow by the Dutch after that.

The British established the federated states, comprising Negeri Sembilan, Selangor, Pahang, and Perak, in 1896. The respective state sultans gave the mandate to the British to have advisors without much **resistance.**

After the Second World War, the British continued their colonialism in Malaya. The British were Malaya's protectorate during the emergence of communist Malaya.

1.3 - British Propaganda

The British twisted the facts and changed their history books. The truth hasn't been told till this day that there were many Malay insurgents within the communists, fighting for independence after the Japanese surrendered. United Malays National Organization (UMNO), for obvious reasons, would not relate the truth till this day about the struggle for independence by fighters like Rashid Maidin, Samsiah Fakeh, Abdullah CD, Dr Burhanuddin, and others.

Rashid Maidin, together with Chin Peng and Chen Tien, met with their British Malayan counterparts, represented by Tunku Abdul Rahman, David Marshall, and Tan Cheng Lok in Baling, in the so-called 'Baling Meeting' in 1955. The agenda, amongst others, was the demand by the communists for the British to leave Malaya and to grant it independence.

However, the British countered the demands by pressuring the communist insurgents to surrender, which caused the negotiation to fail. Do you think Tunku or Tan Cheng Lok had the guts to demand the communists surrender? Do you think the communists were stupid to surrender to the British?

The younger generation is misled about the true history of these events. The true facts of the struggle for independence will be buried in history. Never mind; it is not our interest here.

Those days, post-war students learned from Oxford schoolbooks that the British were here in South-East Asia to trade. They cooked up stories about South-East Asia's spices. As far as we know, Malaya did not have the kind of spices needed for the British to come from thousands of miles away.

Actually, in the sixteenth and seventeenth centuries, the British naval forces, including the Dutch, Portuguese, and Spanish, were competing to find new colonies.

They had military might, which many Asians didn't, so they plundered weaker nations and claimed legal rights. They fought with gunfire, and the weaker nations fought with spirit. What can we expect?

We were made to believe through their books that human origin was from monkeys or apes and the earth was formed from a tiny nuclear cell. These are all nonsense. Actually they were here, amongst other things, on missionary projects to convert Muslims to Christianity. Look at Indonesia, the Philippines, and East Malaysia. Christianity spread like wildfire. The Malays were dump till today. As proof, you can see many Christian schools here still standing. I am not sided anywhere; these are just the facts.

The British were smart. They blended good and bad things to make it look good. Malay youth were taken into the police force to calm the situation. Poor schoolchildren were given scholarships. Children from the elites and royals were sent to England to pursue further education. You see how smart they are? After independence, some students still enjoyed a scholarship until the government changed to student loans.

The British somehow accepted Malay dominance. They retained the respective state sultans, in order to avoid uprisings. The Malays were given special privileges and babysat many of them. The elites were sent to England to study, and upon their return were given top posts in the civil service.

The British protected their tenure by segregating the races by the divide-and-rule policy. The Chinese were driven to homes in towns working as coolies, traders, and shopkeepers. The Indians were sent to rubber plantations, while the Malays were not to be disturbed; they lived in villages or palaces. The educated ones were given work in the civil service.

Uneducated Indians were mostly recruited to work as labourers in town municipal councils. After work, these labourers would get high together on cheap toddy, a coconut-brewed alcoholic beverage sold through the government shop outlets as a preventive measure.

The sales of this brew were taxed under the Customs and Excise. The Chinese lived by their opium world, provided by their underworld clans. Races were kept apart. One was always suspicious of the other.

The segregation policy continues until today. Every race is always suspicious of the other. This race issue is UMNO's trump card to win Malays' support. They will use the race card to checkmate the Chinese rivals on sensitive issues.

1.4 - Malay Supremacy

It was the tragic race riot of 13 May 1969 that triggered the revival of Malay supremacy through its political wing – UMNO. The outcry of Malay supremacy was even more dramatic with the emergence of DAP, a Chinese race-based rival political party. The Malays were under pressure, as DAP had made gains in the recent election. The Malays felt very insecure, and the Chinese were controlling the nation's economy. The Malays rallied under UMNO, which was said to be the protectorate of Malays, their language, and Islam.

The supremacy of the royal monarch is preserved to this day. So the Malay supremacy lives on within the Malay nationalists.

Malays mostly owned property somewhere, somehow, by inheritance or by the grace of the earlier British administration. So the Malays continued to live in comfort through the years. Many had a paddy, rubber, or property. Life was comfortable all the time.

The Chinese were confined to barbed-wire camps built during the British emergency to curb Chinese support for communist Malaya in 1945. They live there to this day. All of them received temporary occupation of said plot of land.

As for the land lot status, today we see factories built on them, legally or illegally. These land lot properties upturned the Chinese economy.

Chinese and Indians worked like crazy for years. The Malays regard them as second-class citizens, as their fathers and grandfathers were migrants who got citizenship by the grace of the local district officer.

The Chinese especially were very enterprising and energetic, unlike the Indians, who had the trademark of the hard-headed toddy drinker. The Chinese do-or-die attitude made them stubborn as mules.

They started small, though. We watched with interest to see them go from selling fish to fruit and from vegetable farming to shopkeepers selling bicycles. Years later we saw Boon Siew's Honda motorcycles in their shop, whilst their Malay friends were still junior officers or police constables in the civil service with wages in small envelopes.

Over the years, these Chinese accumulated wealth for their families and built the economy of the nation as well by paying taxes. The Malays pay taxes too, but much too little, as it is only for the yearly compulsory religious tax 'zakat fitrah' about RM 2.00 a year in those days. (Now it is RM 7.00 a year). Overall the Malays still lag behind, in spite of the effort to improve them by the authority.

1.5 - Malay Nationalism – Unity and Sovereignty

The drive for Malay nationalism occurred in around 1950 as an anti-colonialism struggle. There was strong inclination to uphold the nationalistic idea of creating a Malay nation. The Malay under UMNO, the Malay popular party, struggled to fight on. They won their first election in 1955, and later Malaya was granted independence by the British in 1957.

The sultanate was Malay's oldest known political institution. To this day Malays traditionally submit themselves to the sultans in their respective states. The head of the sultanate is the 'Agong', who is the supreme leader.

The driving force for freedom was peoples' unity and solidarity. Those days from pre-war and after their parents and grandparents had undergone so much suffering and hardship under foreign administration and occupation. The worse experience was under the short reign of the Japanese.

Malays uprising started long ago when the British proposed the Malayan Union to the Malay rulers (there wasn't yet any constitutional that time). The event caused Malays to be united in full force to challenge the British colonialism. Everyone then flagged the banner of unity all over the places. The slogan was indoctrinated in schools, shrines, mosque and public places. Unity was a secret word and was upheld everywhere. The Malays outcry was supported by the Sultans.

The ethnic Malays presently depend very much on UMNO, the hard line Malay political party which currently runs the country. Since the tenancy of UMNO in power it had introduced drastic social and economic reforms to help the 'bumiputeras' ethnic Malays including other ethnics in East Malaysia to lift up their living standards. The New Economic Policy (NEP) is one example of such policies. In spite of the effort made we see nothing gets any better as most of the projects as for example are taken by top members of UMNO and their cronies. The common Dick, Tom and Jerry or Ahmad, Kassim and Awang received nothing, if there is, is only a tiny spill over.

The Sultans and 'Agong' which were said to have supreme authority are now powerless ducklings. They have lost their fangs. Their one time powerful voice had eroded making them sitting ducks in line of fire. They are growing fatter and fatter every day. Many are just puppets on the strings. They have their masters to play the tune to dance.

The country is run by elected Ministers. This bunch of Ali Baba Ministers runs the country at their own perils. Practically everything is controlled by them. Most nations owned Medias paint everything beautiful. Likewise till today many wouldn't understand how and why Singapore, a very strategic Malay island was given away. Further it's weird though why Tanjung Pagar[9], the strategic property owned by Malaysian Railway was sold easily to Singapore.

What happen to the world last Malaysian water tariff to Singapore which is 3 cents per 1,000 gallons. It is very big questionable. If simply cheap sale yours, like your daughters or your mother or your wife (definitely must be pretty enough not like a barrel and must be like that Tanjung Pagar) surely would solve a problem.

I am not sided anywhere, just the fact. It is neither Malaysia nor Singapore.

Malays traditionally and cultural are law abiding citizen. In fact are very, very obedient citizens. Muslim professed utmost loyalty to the elected Ministers as thought by the Quran. They sit obediently under the powerful UMNO authoritarian. These powerful UMNO authoritarian likewise demands undivided loyalty from Malays especially, to be loyal like tame donkeys.

---

9   Tanjung Pagar, Singapore – Let see part 6.6

They lure good corns to induce the donkeys to work. These **obedient** donkeys will strive hard to earn the good corns. In many cases the corn is too far reaching. There is no bite at all.

So far, most Malays uphold this loyalty without questioning. Anyway it must be remembered that;

'Loyalty comes with conditions and disloyalty must come with reasons'. We have read from history book of how the late Sultan Mahmud died. He was stabbed death by his subject for revenge.

The Authorities, on the other hand has the obligation to reciprocate the loyalty given by citizens in equal manner. A notorious robber too, as example, must be fair to his accomplices in order to gain loyalty. He has to show decency and fairness by distributing the loots equally. If he favours one or two of his fellow robbers by giving more loots than others, there will be a revolt. A mutiny will eventually sink the ship.

After World War II there was an outcry for Malay unity to challenge British intervention. There were rallies and uprisings against the British Administrators as the Malays were under pressure from extreme demands from PAP, (that time Singapore was in Malayan domain) the emerging Chinese chauvinist party which were trying to claim for equal rights in citizenship. That was part of the reasons why Tunku Abdul Rahman detached Singapore from Malaya mainland. The emergence of the Communist Malaya after the end of Second World War was worsening the situation. The British finally had to agree to the independence in 1957.

One of the conditions for independence was those Chinese and Indian born here was granted citizenship.

The Malay much regret with the British as during their tenancy of office, they brought in 1.5 million Chinese here. Many worked in British mine yards as labourers. The Indians were also brought in to tend to their rubber plantations. Tin and rubber was important commodity needed by the British that time.

1.6 - Malay Loyalty

Malay loyalty to the supreme authority, the 'Agong' is unquestionable. Same goes with the loyalty to the state Sultans and the elected Ministers running the nation. Its culture and tradition is preserved till this day besides it's the manifest of word of Allah and declared by Prophet Mohammad (peace be upon him) quote:

"He who obeys me, obeys God, he who disobeys me disobeys God. He who disobeys the authority disobeys me" unquote

There is a strong bond between the palace and the Malays. Other races and ethnic have the obligatory responsibility to be loyal to the 'Agong' that is the supreme head and the respective state sultans. Nevertheless many of them shy away because had never been exposed to Malay culture and tradition.

1.7 - Social Life

In general Malays life style has not changed very much. The majority of Malays still lived in isolated village communities. New Palm Oil Township has emerged. Palm oil is currently an important commodity rather than earlier rubber. However families are getting larger and work in villages is getting scarce so many moved to cities to look for open horizon.

Those who live in cities are more exposed to various opportunities. Many Malay now are successful businessmen, engineers, and with some is working in technical professions. They are scattered all over, integrating into various races and ethnics. Lots of them would return home during festival to be united with relatives.

The Chinese seemed to dominate the economy while the uneducated Indians lived in rubber or palm plantations till this day. The educated ones now work as lawyers, doctors or engineers etc.

The Indonesian was the earliest migrants coming from the smaller islands of Indonesia. Many had assimilated in the local community. Foreign aliens namely Banglas (Bangladeshi) and Myanmar now over run the nation like worms, coming in large numbers legally and illegally.

Economically Malays are becoming weaker and weaker by days. Their livelihood is 50 years behind the European and economically 20 years behind the Chinese either. Malays now is about to be outcast citizen of this earth.

Today Malays economy falls back very much behind the Chinese for reasons the later started. Very early in business during which time their (Malay) fathers or grand fathers were busy tending the paddy field or tapping rubber, the Chinese were already active in trading and distribution.

The foreigners, Banglas and Indonesian especially, are draining away the nation's wealth, worse now they are taking away Malay women. And why not, as their ladies, these days, are morally corrupt and Malay men were in hallucination of drug addiction.

The early desperate Chinese were even shrewder. they came here with single pants and shirt, and, out of courtesy, the Malay let them stay in their compound, later they found their way and by sleeping at the porch, demanding more now by eating the food, and later sleep in the room, and later for all we know they were able to check 'the size of the women's underwear' (Malay reserve land[10]). Malays were fools for such extreme patience. It was sheer stupidity. Crazy isn't it.

The Thais, Indonesian or Australian dealt harshly with refugees. Some stubborn ones are even shot down. It's strange that their Immigration allows easy entry to foreigners, so much so now, the locals (Malays) prefer to stay indoor more to avoid mingling with these foreigners.

The irony is the Bangla's' livelihood is better than the Malays in most ways. They are smart and hardworking. They learned Malay language well and adopted Malay cultural fast enough to win Malay ladies. The Malays are dump and stupid as till this day they can't even understand their closeness rivals' language i.e. Mandarin or any of their dialects though born and raised here. There is this saying that Malays stupidity is like killing the goose that lays golden eggs or slaughters their working (ploughing) cow for food.

Everything has gone utterly wrong. As it foreigner had already hauled away billions of dollars since they landed here. The authority has the statistics but kept lips tight for obvious reasons.

The Chinese already, by then, had their chains of business network in the country and overseas. They work well associating with the Small and Medium Industries Association. There are about 3000 Small and Medium Industry members in the country. They complement each member in whatever activities.

In business they treat their own clans differently from Malays or Indians. They regard Malay like stray cat. A Chinese car salesman would look from head to toe for every buyer who comes into his showroom. He would offer to a Chinese buyer a Mercedes or a BMW and he justifies that the car has at top speed of 220 km per hour, as to a Malay buyer he would offer the proton saga and he justifies that the oil consumption is good for Malays, as to the Indians, he would offer 1990 Gallant because he justifies that the car is spacious to load in maximum to 8 passengers more he embarrassed the poor Indians saying the boots are spacious for junks.

---

[10] (One of) The policy to protect the Malay indigenous from outcast

In the current state of socio-economy the Malays are regarded as second class citizens because most Malays are poor. The Indians socially and economically are in no better conditions. Now the Indians cities are better off than the Malays.

Malays are only interested in the small and medium size industries or in small food chain business. Financially Malays depend very much on government support. Nevertheless is difficult to negotiate for financial loans from Government Financial Agencies unless you have some UMNO VIP behind you.

They would prefer to negotiate with Chinese instead. One can understand why. For Malay applicants the process officer would talk cock and giving all the donkey excuses unless under pressure. Many would only provide lips service. Many would follow the Chinese unethical culture - corruption.

Malays are poor pay masters as compared to the Chinese. You would see student loan funds now is almost near exhaustion as not many graduates especially Malays, fail make their payment obligation. Anyway these ex-students would get their way when comes general election. The Malay government would show their generosity. Their payment not very important more than theirs' submit uphold to maintain the premier.

Chinese children started reading book as early as age 4. Their parents send them to tuition classes to study music, play the piano or the violin, or swimming etc. whereas Malay children of same age play kites or spinning tops. Only off late Malay children got addicted with smart phones games online internet.

Chinese parents invest heavily on their children. One thing we cannot deny that the Chinese are good in mathematic whereas most Malay children hate mathematics. Their children are indoctrinated with business mind set to continue their parents' or grandparents' legacy. They realize the urgency to turn around business quickly. The Malays had choices and do not have the urgency and they are very selective.

Malays live mostly live in villages off the city while the Chinese lives in city suburb. Early morning Malays wake up to see green, green, green environment which makes them fresh but sleepy, whereas the Chinese wake up to see the world go round. They see the dollar sign in their eyes.

There is the need to keep up Malays to current living standard in order to maintain social. The Malays will continue to be loyal to UMNO for the sake of Malay supremacy.

PART 2.0 - TYPICAL ATTITUDE

2.1 - Common Practice

Those days there are a lot of good practices in Malay culture. Now a day most are wipe-off vanished. Leave nothing and changing to bad petty things.

They are too vulnerable to any bad culture outside, promiscuously.

There are a lot, amongst that are;

- Non religiously (mainly)
- No clarity
- Too much amusement and wasting time
- Shallow in thinking and over proud
- Non-professional and discipline on leadership
- Recently is wickedness

Empty, moral corrupted, talk big and keen to cheat and steal on anything even as small as ball pen, eraser, kitchen knife, much more if camera.

Very like to show off especially on power, practically it is very small.

The hard-headed 'principle' that always on the most Malay mind especially in bureaucrat and some Malay related institutions is;

- <u>'How to make trouble'</u> to anybody they deal with in order to show their existence or power. Small example but actually not small; 'Purposely' now a great confusing all over the nation of every second then times a million of peoples they make 20 cents and 50 cents coin almost same size and colour, so with 5 cents and 10 cents.
  - o What for if it is earlier better? To shows his existence and to justify for his 'haram' (it mean forbidden in Islam) salary for not doing anything? End up worse now – create mishap and getting money. They knock our head then we pay for that. The real bustard! Their existence is to be outcast. That is what we had in the country.

o   Back ward mentality is not possible maybe, and then only thing
    is 'wicked' or stupid due to never get exposure like in Malay prose
    '*Katak di bawah tempurung*'[11]

o   How they practice their religious contribution to make a million of
    peoples in troublesome? Islamic faith thought, a good or bad thing
    it will be 'a particle' count and to be answered in the Day After.

o   This kind of small thing (coin matter) it supposes not to call any
    intention at all. It means fingers will automatically 'works' without
    mistakes. How small the thing is was
    'seconded' by this old Nokia (2008)
    'Battery full. Unplug charger to save
    energy.' It is how small energy is[12]?
    Then it is comply with Islamic faith
    and universal – save energy. Where
    the Muslim of Malays is?

o   In industrial practice, there are
    procedures to make design or
    situation to avoid stupid mistake
    and great famous Japanese word is
    'Pokayoke'[13]

o   Don't be trifle with 'particle' size as
    Muslim thought and all civilized peoples are. After long calculation,

    ▪ 'The introduction of the redundant machine reduces quality
       cost by $0.086 for each product, or $258,000 per year' (Taguchi,
       1989, p. 138). That is how the small thing works for factories
       and how about if country scale[14]? Medium size factory manager

---

[11] The frog is under coconut shell. It mean he thought his world 'that so big'

[12] If a few millions of phone sets over the world, how many tons of carbon yielded per
      annum? There are a lot of talk about green effect and lead to the creation of 'carbon
      trading' (find the fair solution alternatively to poor and rich countries) in order to
      balance and to help the world as a whole. Then how precious they are comparing to
      the Muslim Malay born by inheritances?
      • Practically now converted Muslim images and personalities will closer to Islamic
         faith rather than deviated born Muslim Malay.

[13] This word I got and understand from Perodua Automobile staff – Amzar.

[14] Country scales and it's time value – The Malay clan! Do you understand this? Listen!
      In 1970iest Tambak Johor (passage over trouble water Johor to Singapore) was
      collecting one million dollars per day. It was 40 over years before and the value of
      money that time graduate bureaucrat getting about 750 dollars and primary school

in Singapore easily can manage this country for about 100 times better than any UMNO leader now.

- Clever wise man is always thinking to make easiest way to the people, establish a simple routine.
- The routine and system which an efficient executive establishes enable an average person to perform tasks which previously only a very capable person could do. In fact the test of a good executive is to make ordinary people achieve extraordinary performance' (M.K.Rustomji, 1986, p. 3)

- <u>'How to fail this thing'</u> promiscuously constantly. Verbally none but on the practice will shows. It is must be suffer and torture to deal with. You not even finish the word he already dissenting.
- <u>'Create lengthy'</u>. It is about one inch or two but they will create until it becomes ten and maybe hundreds for wasting times and waste everything. Furthermore it is very hateful like nothing to do (maybe as above, to justify he had something done for taking his salary).
  - o For example last time the word only *'baru'* (it means 'new') but now it should say *'baharu'*. Since Y generation like to simplify anything in communication like sending message even jot a lecture note. All those days we had 'short-hand' courses for what? …
- Most of people don't like it – backward mentality. In Muslim as above 'a particle' will accounted for. It is spending more and wasting time. Everybody doesn't like to wait and queue in line isn't it? That is why in Malaysia it is quite normal the people violent 'red' and 'yellow' in traffic light – don't like to wait.
  - o Their faith, Prophet Muhammad will talk little only and very compact don't like wasting time at all. His time is very precious. Then consequences there is a lot of elaboration of 'hadith'[15] to land out a thousand and thousands of *'kitab'* (can consider as special books-preaching). Then we saw the emergence of 'mazhab' (school of thought) due to differentials. Albeit so many difference opinions but it is not in principle.

---

teacher (colleges) are getting three hundred and ten dollars for starting salary. Now how much to imagine the financial mishap to the country.

[15] His (Prophet Muhammad) words and behaviour.

They really struggle for a good post to be a civil servant. This is the most secure from any aspect, especially least commitment to the responsibility. Whoever tries to work as what it should be, he is against the 'current flow nature' and will land him in trouble. If they don't want to do their own certain task, they also don't want other people do otherwise become enemy. Heart and soul of majority Islamic Malay – wicked!

That why at the early stage, Mahathir 'cannot use finance ministerial department' properly. Aggressively he cannot wait and alternatively he used Economic Planning Unit until Daim (ex-Finance Minister) reconstitute and utilise it.

Actually it is easy to understand; The Malay doesn't want to change. They want to maintain 2015 as 1950's to keep 3 or 5 chicken, go to fishing for two or three fishes in near riverside and lean on tree trunk.

So that why lengthy. But somehow rather they still want to use smartphone, tablet and all up to date thing. They also want to stylish in Pizza Hut, KFC or McDonald.

I wish to elaborate the common Malays attitude when I was freelance service maintenance technician servicing SIRIM (Malaysian standard body) in Sepang. One incident there was a part replacement required for data acquisition (actually computer) of Canada origin. (It was wrongly fixed due setting to Malaysian standard power grid, 240v by the Canadian Engineer during installation).

After hassling and searching for its spare parts, I found out it's should refer to the agent Hewlett Packard. HP had records of product sold by them. It was HP who traced product from its serial number to identify the machine parts.

---

16   Both - ZP's collection, 2004, Sirim Sepang

Really it's very simple, just from it serial number, the counter girl (not supervisor, manager and so on) counter back to confirm is the equipment bought in Canada. Purely complete and final solution, "the equipment is new not in Malaysian market yet. You need to order for us to get it from UK or US."

2.1.1 - FIVE MINUTES SESSION

Everything is in their hand. Their worldwide information just on finger tips. We no need to tell the particulars such as date of purchase, warranty period and a lot of grandmother stories in thick 'bible'. They straight go to 'action step'. If applicable to warranty, we no need even talk or request it. Less than 5 minutes session.

This is the......

2.1.2 - 'WORLD STANDARD'.

We heard the first problematic Prime Minister, Abxxxxxx Baxxxx that time barking, shouting and howling on air daily promoting Malaysia being best emerging industrial nation and we are in the world standard. It is embarrassing to talk nonsense.

2.1.3 - EMPTY TALK

It's Malays habit to be captive to prejudice, preconception, and pre-judgment of things around. They would go round and round beating the bush discussing small irrelevant and unrelated matters. Definitely like this HP (Canada-SIRIM things), staffs about 4 or 6 even managers would gather until lunch for example to walk the talk about the machine all day relentlessly. They would enjoy complimenting each other with empty talk to take time away. Nothing is substantial.

It was sickening to see them doing nothing to improve the inventory or storage system as for example as the same thing happening over and over again. There was no clear course in it. Other institutions like FELDA, FELCRA, NEB, and TV3 were doing much better. There was no clarity in the purpose of their employment.

2.1.4 - LOOSED LIPS

Malays, unlike the Chinese, have loosed lips. One can be persuaded by sweets. Gentle talk, ladies, money and gifts make them walk the talk. Some weaker ones just need a cup of coffee to talk. It is sheer weaknesses and greed. He could be telling secrets to almost everyone he meets until the secrets are no more secrets.

Malays are weak as they had been suppressed by those in power for years. They are naïve as they are misled by unclear teaching of Islam as their own religious. It looks as though there are two sets of Islam profess by two Malays influential political parties, namely the nationalist UMNO and the Islamist Pan Islamic Party. Their fanatic follows often the clash on Islamic fundamental issues.

2.1.5 - CONTENTED, SLOW CHANGING & VENERABLE

Malays couldn't move fast enough to anticipate with the changing environment unlike the Chinese who could adjust with the changes. Many are still detached from the outside world. ASTRO, smart phone and internet are considered a luxury them, the only information they have is the nation run media with which its intellectual information is very limited … their weaknesses are easy target for UMNO to capture the hearts and minds to continue their reign.

Current 'Malay' government is always nervous when Election Day comes. Malay would be expected to receive a windfall of goods. Their armies swarm like bees covering large areas even to remote villages distributing 'sarung' a women piece wear, sugar, rice bags etc.[17]

Malays are venerable to such tactics. That's how UMNO maintain power since independence. But until when they can keep so long 2015 as 1950.

Malays leaders do not have the guts to go for change. It is talks only. They are contented with what they are. It's living in comfort zone. There were attempts by some aggressive groups to go for change but their attempts were short lived. There are many devils in disguise living amongst them. Attempt to progress usually is blocked by some apple polishers or sycophants sticking around to top officials.

---

[17]　ZP's collection, 2013, Pekan Pahang

2.1.6 - WASTING TIME, OVER-COST PRODUCTIVITY, ASTRAY

Malays with pea heads are fond of deviating away from the topics and starts talking shits, out of their grandmother's tail. That is the problem. Malay institutional meetings are done so often, so much so, as if they have all the time on this planet. They will have meetings after meetings - to fix the meeting date, there must be a meeting, or several post meetings then there will several after post meetings and other several meetings and meetings God knows what before the actual meetings.

For what we know for breakfast or lunch one will enjoy good roasted chicken, sweet sour grouper 'kerapu' and some cash and other perks. The Chairman uses his authority the way he likes. When the Chairman greets a long 'salaaaam' it would mean the meeting is adjourned. What a joke? Then they will be busy collecting bills to submit all types of claims … This is typical habit of the Malays in Malay organization – it is non-productive.

To quote Lee Kuan Yew's words about meeting. He said "storm over a coffee cup"- he meant no essence. the meeting is non- productive, just coffee session, talk about family matters, show of at family's album and hook-up family photograph in the office.

We have to accept the fact that this has been their 'world standard culture', the Malays benchmark, unlike in the commercial sector, the young educated breeds show much better responsibility. They are more productive.

I was trained in industrial and moral discipline found it odd to see irrelevant and often lengthy walk the talk without clarity. Many things should be brief and result oriented. Previously letters (especially Malay correspondences) were written in very poetic and often with bombastic and flamboyant words and languages with no clarity however now, letters are done simple in blocks with message directed to the purpose of such letters.

Typical example is the postal mails in the States.

CA 94034, it mean California or MA 37039, it mean Massachusetts etc.

The addresses of mails are short and brief.

Undoubtly Malaysia long time ago has adopted such format, nevertheless it needs to refine and to educate the people to understand the purposes.

I agreed with postcode Malaysia Postal Services which a letter address should be short and brief. Like existing now for example:

42500 Telok Panglima Garang

Short brief and easy readable. It helps the post officers to ease (sorting) the work load quicker. A brief training is sufficient for new postal staffs or volunteers to handle the work load efficiently. Malaysian is well versed with towns and cities like Jitra is related to Kedah; Lenggong in Perak but Lenggeng in Negeri Sembilan; Kubang Gajah in Perlis but Alor Gajah in Malacca, Batu Kikir in Negeri Sembilan but Batu Arang-Selangor.

In my opinion Postal addresses should be like now, short and brief with code number and town, underline, no comma or a full stop, and for the state like Kedah should omit Darul Aman, or Perlis omit Indra Kayangan or Pahang omit Darul Makmur.

In my opinion, it would help postal man a lot, otherwise he has to spend more money for eye treatment or medicated salon plaster to avoid migraine. It's time a standardize address format be introduced like the printed Express mail envelopes. In my opinion, time has come to educate the public to anticipate with the application of to-days technology.

Postal services should be more apply electronic systems like using postal scanner for assembling and sorting of letters as they did with Poslaju Services. Therefore envelopes should be designed electronically for such purposes.

It is something to consider, the philosophy of road traffic sign. A brief compact and fast 'explanation' to drivers is good for the most of people except Malay clan.

Do you like a people talking to you for about half an hour just to borrow ball pen to tick of missing in check-box? Or the above, the driver must stop, facing to sign-board, has a drink and study 'the essay' what it mean by the road traffic order?

TO ALL MALAYS JUST THINK OF IT!

Another example for redundancy

Malays are fond to skid fall of the function of their name which sometimes not serve the purpose. They like to have glamorous identities, like names and nick names. Such typical flamboyant name which we see today like:

Puteri Intan Baiduri Irama Mendayu Seri Wangi Di Malam Jumaat binti Abu.

So long name you need to ask, how to call. Eventually the father's name just 3 letters, A,b,u. To be fair since the first last 30 over years all of my children's name just consist 5 letters.

What's the purpose?

Two things will happen to this girl when she grows up and found it's the work of their parents. She would feel silly or glamorous. Those feeling silly ones will feel confuse like her parents as by then nothing much one could do. The glamorous one, on the other hand, will be the star, the talk of talk of the town. Probably she will be on record world Guinness Book of record.

Such lengthy name does not serve the purpose. It makes life complicated to everyone. Printers have to introduce new form for such names, even computer system too can go bust - break down. All in all it doesn't serve the purpose. Why you must cheat yourself. Straight forward and self-explanation (if needed) is better.

This expensive high speed sport car yet not carry lengthy name. The Lamborghini family name it as 'Diablo'[18]. Diablo mean devil in Spanish and maybe due to high speed like devil 320km/h. All of all it is self-explanation.

The problems of Malays are there are easily influences by odd things. Long or Alley Cat hair type is said to be fashioned. Can anyone explain those wearing mask like Zorro (Amok). Is that fashion too? In my opinion it is the craziest thing beyond redemption.

2.1.7 - OVER PROUD

This is the biggest problem of Malay and they don't want to change[19]. If they have less than 1 inch they will brag like they have a yard or even more than a kilometre especially if they are in 'government' or related to government. The issue may be very small but they inflate, ridiculously bubble-up boast up to show like he is the biggest and the fiercest on the planet.

I would like to brief one latest good example on myself, about one well known telecommunication company[20], of course related to Malay or at least in the hand of Malay 'executive power'[21].

Whoever not interested, please skip to the following.

I was subscribing since 1991 it is about 25 years. That times the service only in Klang Valley. Hand phone set is about RM6,000 (Car phone, Mobira is about

---

[18] You can surf in internet.

[19] Whoever try to admonish or advice, they will be the greatest enemy. Their hell-bent at all cost to upright their wrong, must, must and must be agreed. Actually like a Malay prose itself they like to up-right a wet thread (cotton). Definitely they are no shame and non-professional at all.

[20] I'm very thankful for this top best real example case. It is in the nick of time of my needed. It is not simply pluck in the air or by assumption through experience. Then you all can think how much hassle created by them every day. By right if they obey their Islamic rule (a good human being is who make good for others), they were rewarded continuously and unlimited by the God – very easy 'RICH' in the Day After. Malay the stupid clan! Their today (life) and the Day After are gone together.

[21] At this level in this story

RM14,000 – nationwide inclusive in jungle normally very useful in logging camp). Advance deposit on subscribing was RM300 fixed there. They can put fixed deposit in the bank. If they had one million subscribers, then RM300 million could be in FD. An access fee is 'beheaded' for RM60 per month. It means zero airtime. Call charge is 30 cents per minute. The services are very poor – line very busy[22]. Normally average people will spend about RM300 to RM500 for monthly bill. Just for information, that time a technician or senior clerk salary is about RM500 per month i.e., one year flat salary for such basic hand phone and a full month salary just for phone bill only. Fresh diploma graduate is about RM400 per month. Indeed that all you agree to subscribe, not a matter. It is just to show how the long stayers endurance 'swim and sink' together with the company.

My recent experience, please scrutinise the following messages (SMS).

---

1) SMS – Credit Limit <u>This is 05/10/2016 at 15:22hrs</u>

RM0 To suit yr usage pattern, Cexxxx offer a crdt limit increase fr 500 to 650. Send YES to accept/NO to decline to 28889 w/in 24hrs. Info☐ial 1111.T&C

Sender:
(no name)
Cexxxx

Received:
15:22:29
05/10/2016

---

22   If nearby I always line up for public phone booth and my RM6,000 Technophone will put on auto redial. Mostly after 20 callers clear their call on phone booth then only I get my call. Sometime I need to use that public phone only. There one funny experience, I call from KL and drive until Klang get into the office then talk face to face. The phone is still unable to connect. Driving is faster?

2) SMS - <u>This is 21/11/2016 at 10:02hrs</u>

Kindly note yr bill amount RM 134.35 is ovedue. Pls mk pymt within 7 days to avoid call barring. Pls disregard this msg if pymt made. Bill info: dial*111#.TQ

Sender:
(no name)
Cexxxx

Received:
10:02:58
21/11/2016

3) SMS - <u>This is 25/11/2016 at 09:12hrs</u>

RM0 Thank you for your payment of RM100.00. Stay connected with Cexxxx!

Sender:
(no name)
Cexxxx

Received:
09:12:06
25/11/2016

4) SMS - <u>This is 26/11/2016 at 10:50hrs</u>

Kindly note yr bill amount RM 34.35 is ovedue. Pls mk pymt within 1 day to avoid call barring. Pls disregard this msg if pymt made. Bill info: dial*111#.TQ

Sender:
(no name)
Cexxxx

Received:
10:50:09
26/11/2016

> **5) Call - <u>This is my call Monday 28/11/2016 at 20:00hrs</u>**
>
> 1111
> Time of call
> 20:00:16
> 28/11/2016
>
> Call duration
> 00:13:40
>
> Note: <u>*I made this call after I know my line was barred.*</u>
> <u>*Answered by Noor (sound likely must be Malay lady)*</u>

I threw my tantrum hoping they catch my bait and thud in trap[23]. Done!

This is not first unethical troublesome. Only thing this is their extremely stupid bad image and very shameful reflex to my clan. No brain! Then it is my fully right to stand-up for my clan and 'kills' traitors if necessary.

- Just because of these 34 dollars and 35 cents they cut the line of my long stay more than 25 years? Arrogantly response like hooligan. Ten fingertips must upward to them as we are paying?
- My credit limit is RM500, had been offered to increase to RM650 due to my usage pattern.
- I check up to date (plus unbilled) total is ±RM250
- I was in rural area (where I stay) had to jump up 85km to Kuantan? Just after 3 days paid (100 out of 134.35 demanded)[24] in town? They think all subscribers (getting the money from the sky) must surround the paying machine like beggars to feed them 24/7/365. Better still telling the truth if you are going to bankrupt, no money to pay salaries then we understand and rush up to pay any debt even it is 35 cents or maybe advancement another 65 cents.
- Their normal practise.....
  - o   21st Nov – request 134.35 (within 7 days)

---

[23]   It is the right time material for my writing. Rigid and detail case. Nothing wrong as it is their wicked and normal practice – happily to make troublesome to customers.

[24]   It is about this time I make payment progressively like piggy bank; not only one payment per month.

o 25th Nov – paid 100.00 (accepted by SMS)

o It is enough until next month. Most of subscriber did it through a machine like this.

o On 28th Nov – they bar the line for 34.35

o Normally is not like this. If my bill is 300 and I pay 200 (through machine) it is enough until next month. Furthermore in the middle of interval I pay the balance of that 100 to avoid accumulation. So it means those of them (Malay officers) always developing and thinking progressively how to make troublesome to others and hoping to regard them powerful. Toward Satanic will and against to their Islamic faith.

To all the readers what the reaction you guess?

Yesssssssssss....... They are look for 'fighting' to show off their arrogant rather than business. My subscribing history maybe is older than their age. Pity their corporate.

After one hour, instead of the apology (May through SMS) and connect back my line (very simple and it doesn't varnish the amount isn't it?[25] Creating more in bill as I am still using the phone), they throw their tantrum (to extremely long stay customer – since that time their system only have 6 digit analogue and starting 010). Now everything was recorded here to tell the world how stupid they are toward the Malay outcast.

Everybody can see here? They put 150.95 instead of original 34.35 within one hour. They are killing and their 'master' duties are stripping out customers.

I must admit they are BIG and now they are happily laughing complement each other to celebrate 'the world success trophy' then special holiday plus dinner of lamb chop or chicken chop plus shark fins maybe for whole week. That is the most bureaucrat and government link companies' Malay culture.

---

[25] Do you think this subscriber will run with that amount and very long sentiment history to vanish?

6) SMS - <u>This is 28/11/2016 at 21:07hrs</u>

Kindly note that u hv an outstanding bill of RM150.95. Pls mk pymt as yr may hv been barred.U can still dial*111# or 1111 for assistance.TQ

Sender:
(no name)
Cexxxx

Received:
21:07:28
28/11/2016

How come they to be like this?

If I haven't made that call, throw my anger (facing them with all fingers up right) definitely I just to pay 34.35 then line will be connecting back. Somehow rather I acquire right chance, take all risk and did the right thing for the sake of customers[26]. Let the company go to hell if they really need it.

I cannot refrain anymore as their service gradually worse and this is extremely unimagined super stupid case[27]. 101% their mistake and should apology. I do expect what is going to be when I throw my tantrum. Only thing I am wrong with some deviate. I thought they will bounce back within 10 minutes but it happen about one hour and I thought it going to impose me straight to RM250 but it only RM150.

---

[26]   Can you guess if you complaint and anger to a service of high class hotel even how right they are and how wrong you are? How they handle and solve the problem? They bounce back and punch you on their own yard? Malay executive should learn to live in the real globe *(especially customer is always right)* or just be a coolie or bouncer *(take care of Chinese pub and night club)* or outcast with their own trade mark drug addiction.

[27]   I have no wrong at all as my assumption they have no work other than chewing peanut *(the most I hate – in front of customers, while one hand holding the packet and the other one picking the nut. This is not going to be happen if they works with Chinese corporate like Hong Leong group, why?. That automatically showed this clan could be just coolies)* and with full brain effort how to treasonous customers not even look how stupid the case is, promiscuously.

Some of my friends ask me to follow them to change the 'system'. I just keep quite. They also long stay like me but I never ask why.

o   One of my close friends (019-3361xxx) also registered in 1991 jump out sometime ago. He only said a lot of problem, no customers oriented, they don't want customers. Everywhere (other than Malay oriented) is "Our valued customer.......", "without you all we are no business". Very humble Chinese businessmen and don't care how small[28] you are in his business. In fact he has one fleet of new Mercedes difference series and the youngest daughter drive Honda sport to college. Ungrateful, they shit out to us as we are paying them, their survival; they want our fingertips upward to them like a king. They think they can stand alone. Go to Hell they are. Just beetle off laa....Zul".

As usual Malay don't know and don't want to learn proper business, the company should turn (sell) to non-Muslim better. Put a big sign 'Malay properties' even not a single cent equity then hue and cry – "we are the biggest, top challenging we are first corrupted in the world". Still the winner isn't it?

My statement is in compliance to ex Menteri Besar (Chief Minister) of Selangor. Tan Sri Khalid defence his standing on appointment of PKNS (state economic development authority) acting general manager - October 2008.
    '...........between loss of a few billion dollars in the hand of Malay and earning few million in non-Malay hand'
    It is very easy out. No more dilemmas. Mahathir was tried out for more than 20 years. Totally failed! Bureaucrats turn back to as before. No more clock card on 08:00 to start a job[29], very big hassle. No more customers' oriented.

---

28   They never realise how politician raise up need every single vote to become president or Prime Minister. Even Islamic preaching the God will count up to 'particle' of good and bad.
29   They forget their obligation is to their God, not Mahathir. God will count to particle. If you swore to start your job at 08:00, obligation to the God is like that.

2.2 - Corruption-Rampant

2.2.1 - CIVIL SERVICE - CORRUPT PRACTICES

Now days the practices like to be almost open task and talk, anytime and anywhere. It's doesn't matter how stupid you are, you will 'smell' it. It would be all level from top highest to very low bottom like 'pariah' country.

These are just sharing of three stories;

2.2.1.1 - Close Shop!

Probably last 15 years I had to buy something for Windmill Project in Pasir Gudang Johore. The hardware shop had been asked whether the part is genuine. The shop-keeper stand-up with eyes and hands wide open with high pitch;

"Why you ask like that? We never sell non genuine part. All traceable record was here. Once mistake "Closeddd shop! oahh (with hands axed). Don't play afoul."

That shows the integrity of the law enforcement and everybody scared.

Off late in the same shop and keeper,

"Hai yaa … Naxxx maa.., 20 dollars can settle maa … …"

Now all over the country was flooded by that quality of goods. They mean third class and rejected quality brought by underwear and taxi's tyre brainchild.

Brand new TV set, it is just for 3 or 4 months and then another 3 or 4 months in workshop for warranty. Wonderful! Very clever they can make such quality of goods (problem will arise within 3 of 4 months). Then come out for a few months follow by another problem and the warranty period almost lapse.

For a watches batteries it's 10 dollars just for 2 or 3 weeks rather than 1 or 2 years last time. Then offer better one for 18 dollars. It is just exactly one month. It is really the country rotten to the core by the Malay leadership.

Purely printed 'Made in Germany' (Last time only the word of 'Germany') is not Germany, other shop in Northern states, Kedah.

"Hai yaa … the goods they can make, to print like that cannot?"

So … the core also rots. Everything falls down. ♩London Bridge♫ falling♪ down♫♫ … ♩London Bridge♫ falling♪ down♫♫ …

2.2.1.2 - Death Certificate.

One old man in Kedah expressed out disappointed after getting 'Death Certificate' of his mother (or his father?). He needs to come until four times and almost taken 2 month period just for them to tear off a letter (that certificate). He comes about 12 miles away with very old motorcycle (more than 30 years old).

He must leave his job 3 times for non-productive one. That also after he raises the voice and starts angry. "Do you all need other people come and take my death certificate then?" Otherwise he maybe needs to go for a few times more. Pity the old sincere man. He doesn't know maybe they need to be hand shaking with money inside, let say maybe 2 or 3 dollars.

That is how suffer to become current citizen, extremely very low 'pariah' class of the world's corrupted country.

If you buy a towel, it looks like towel but it is plastic/acrylic (no absorption). Lucky for EU country they have certain standard to pass through. This country now becomes the rubbish dump of mainly China products. Anything you want to throw, you can dump in Malaysia and they pay for that. They like to give baton to knock their head and don't worry they will pay for that.

2.2.1.3 - Midnight traffic Light.

This is another story still in Johor for last 2 or 3 years, somewhere in Masai.

This Chinese hardware shop owner is very familiar with me. He had a last night story to tell me.

It is about 2.00 am he hasn't stop for 'red' traffic light. It is very clear traffic and historically that place quite danger for you to stop that time – robbery.

He saw two policemen with small motorbike hiding and start chasing him after. Then he is simply slow to let them approach him to stop.

They (policemen) start talking so many stories. To cut short,

"I have money and can give you how much you want, 10, 20, 30, 50, 100, 200?" He rises up his voice.

He continues, "You know that place is very danger about this time, most of the drivers will not stop. That why you waiting there isn't it? I can stop no problem. The problem is both of you. You listen! You just about twenty plus. You want to start practise thisssss,….. until retire?, what will happen to you? How your mothers and fathers teach you? Are you Muslim?..........................."

Those two policemen just keep quiet and beetle off the guy to continue his driving. Their attempt failed.

What would this world can be benefit of those two Malay guys? It is definitely eligible for outcast?

Life just like vulture scrum for carcass or like a rats live in leachate in rubbish dump or housing area.

2.2.1.3.1 - 'Syariah' Court Lawyers

If we look higher up some 'syariah' court[30] lawyers' just petty fogger and some judges will sell their dignity to the dog. How much? Yeah… as low as three thousand dollars they simply booked one of the Hell's 'genuine key'.

What they learn in universities? Maybe how to create easy money by riding on Islamic law practising and repent later? They know when to die?

Unfortunately there was nothing to hinder them not likes those two policemen. Pity them, everything run smoothly to the hell because they are undoubtedly holding the Islamic flag along their way.[31]

2.3 - Erratic Policies

It's usual when there is revamp in the cabinet, there will change in policies. The new Ministers like empty tank to show he is somebody would introduce new unproven systems for example the education system.

Parents got confuse of the erratic policies implemented by the ministry. The syllabuses are chaotic.

In 70's there were compulsory examinations for student to universities. Their minimum standard would the Cambridge Higher School Certificate with two years extension from normal School Certificate. Two years extra would mean two years smarter and mature.

Now university intakes were depend on good marks in the School Certificate. So we would see are immature undergraduate in universities. They are not capable to project maturity. Further they can't speak proper English what more to read Oxford or Cambridge English books.

2.3.1 - EXAMPLE (ENGLISH SUBJECT)

While working on ship maintenance anchorage in international water (the South China Sea), I am facing communication problem.

---

30 'Syariah court' it mean Islamic legislation court of justice
31 For further story please refer to 7.4 – 'Syariah' Court

Many technical staffs include the newly grad engineers were not proficient in English. So how could it be possible to discuss technical matters as the operating manuals are all in English? Strange isn't it.

It is evitable, whether one likes it or not, that English language is important. The Chinese have at least three languages namely Chinese language (with various dialects), Malay and English. Malay guy speak they understand. They curse the Malay nod and giggle because they do not understand. Its look silly isn't it?

The attempt to better education in English by sending students over sea is a good idea. Malaysian government is doing it discreetly for obvious reasons. Upon return many will resume executive posts strictly in the civil service sector. That's not a good idea. More should be assimilated to the private sectors where they can be trained in commerce and industry.

Off late there are lots of controversies with using English language for teaching and learning in science and mathematics which it acronym is PPSMI. The Ministry still not settle its direction. There was lot s of public outcry on this matter. In many cases teachers and parents have to play dump; otherwise they will be stamped as traitors. The linguistic specialists in DBP are just like Persian cats –expecting everyone to comply with what they do. Contented to what they have.

---

[32] All 3 - ZP's collection, 2008; South China Sea

2.3.2 - MONKEY PLAY

School education syllabuses are just like monkey play. The non-stop subjects feeding all in one go is choking the students. Standard six students now have to carry truckloads of books to school. Parents on the other hand have to earn extra by working overtime for children's tuitions.

Parents whose children studying abroad have fewer headaches because school syllabuses are more or less fix for the rest of the year. Their semester holidays are strictly their private holidays. Holiday is holiday (Is there any holiday is not holiday?). That the very basic word 'holiday' the Malaysian authorities not understand.

Those day world class psychologists and sociologists was study the behaviour and the necessity of 'rest' and its periodic for human being as what the teachers was learn in the colleges. One nobody can deny is daily rest, it is 'sleep'. What happen if anybody wakes up with good sleep?

If students in abroad fail certain paper, they will have time to get revision even look for tuition. My schooling time it was same. If any poor subject, part of holiday will become 'punishment'. Somehow rather it's normally not more than 20% of holiday. That time the holiday is the time to throw the books. Relax and broadly open your horizon, see what happening outside and help your parents.

If one can thinks they can compare to Muslim fasting month every year. That can consider as brake or holiday for too much eating. After that you can feel 'fresh' and start back again.

Back to abroad if everything ok, they can work for additional money for their study by sending pizza, work in restaurants etc. the key was 'holiday' to ensure when you back to study it will be 'fresh', stimulate with new spirit.

Teachers and students here usually got bogged down with school work even on holidays. The disappointing thing is in spite of the time spent on them, they don't get any better. Just enough, simplicity should be better. Overload/over tighten for the screw will loose and everything fall down.

During my childhood, students like me had more time to spend with our parents. Many could help the family during school holidays meaning to say children got closer to parents. Parents was able to pass their trades, like planting rice, or even tapping rubber in the estate or picking cocoa or palm in the plantation.

However now children with full load of home-works don't even understand what parents mean to them as they are practically don't have time for even to cook rice with rice cooker or to wash underwear with washing machine. What this generation can promise to themselves as to run daily life they can't. In the last time you can get maid. Earlier time maybe you can get slave. Today in Malaysia you must depend on yourselves as the maid if any become a 'boss'.

Seeking employment with academic certificate alone is not easy in the commercial sectors now. The private sector needs candidates with trade knowledge and discipline. It looks now there are efforts to pass trades and technical training to 'y' generation. Too many sycophants – hindering progress

2.4 - Wild Thinking – Craze, Greed

An unethical contractor could secure RM 1 m bridge project inflated to RM 10 m. The devil inside him induced him to spin figures, spin people, and spin the authorities to satisfy his ends. We would catch everybody by the horns. Why so? He carries three wives and each expects to own one bungalow and or sport cars. On top of that his devil head looks for the prospect of taking another wife – the dowry could be heavy this time. The oldest wife needs at least an Alphard to sign off the marriage application.

He cooks lies to everyone on top of that he would have more wild day dreams how to manipulate further, perhaps to get stronger contact from VIPs as for instance. He is prepared to take more risks and the consequences. His devil head comfort himself saying he has contingencies comforting himself. So the project of RM1 m after conversion and making various provisions tilted one side - inflated to RM15 m to cover kick back, inducement and to oiling the whole system.

How one could justifies such absurd figure. Any stupid and dump person can smell rat. It is such a 'terror' type of person plundering the nation in broad daylight. Such person if he walks past the grave of Sphinx, this devil too have his eyes wide open, and if he walks past the mummy of Pharaoh, that mummy will stand up give axed salute - most notorious devil after his era.

PART 3.0 - COMMERCE MALAYSIA PERSPECTIVE

3.1 - Small Businesses

Business activities in villages namely fishing village are badly hit by short of labour.

Domestic production of *'belacan'* prawn shrimp cake (by pounding) now is about 20 pieces/day as there are not many who are interested to work. Previously it was something like 30 pieces. Many educated ones left and migrated to cities for obvious reasons. Good ones are too old to do the pounding.

There are efforts to restructure such businesses to more productive type. The Small and Medium Industries activities are being set up especially for the Malays' benefit.

However, the Malays in villages are slow to adopt new technologies unlike the Chinese or Banglas (Bangladeshi) who practically dominated big and small businesses even in remote areas.

It's unethical to condemn my own clans but it remains a fact that the clans are hopeless. They are not ready to accept new things and new challenges. They have all sorts of excuses some our beyond imagination. They would say money is jinx. Some other will quote a proverb 'one pot of rice will never be two pots' some others will have some sorts of unrealistic excuses.

For those who have sleepy head or a dreamer would want to maintain its classical production methods for sentimental reasons which are should be in showcase. It's their cow dung head saying so. Actually they are not enterprising enough like the Banglas (Bangladeshi) or the Indonesian who migrated here. These foreigners now turn becomes 'bosses' of their own businesses already employing local workers in their enterprises. The worse thing is again there are some devils like the head or village committee head who simply hate to see others flourish unless they can benefit somehow one way or another.

Actually Malays are always contented with what they are, living in comfort zone. They are not far sighted. they have the 'wait and see' attitude until such time their women are taken away by Banglas only then they will be busy sharpening with their short curvy blades and chanting like real warriors. Cow dung head!!!

All in all it's about attitude-Malay relaxing attitude. Relax and sing until dooms day.

3.2 - Sustainable Development

Many communities are still left unattended. They grow at very slow pace. There are poor infrastructure villages. So much so many village youths move to city suburb for employment.

It is unfair for government to favour just around KL and major towns. Even though the most important thing is congested and cramp.

It is heavy load on every aspect of town life. It's better to distribute and share with the outskirt. Some new town-ship maybe better especially for who not really related to the particular town let say proven best example, the new emerges of Putrajaya rather than stay in KL; international airport in Sepang rather than still in Subang; administration Washington D.C. rather than commercial New York.

I sees prospect to develop Muadzam and Pekan-Rompin area, such infrastructure is necessary to move the village's forwards toward the new centurion. The authority or its representative should find the solution to develop new township in prime villages like Muadzam, Pekan-Rompin.

The infrastructure is - Railway track 3 degree horizontal north KL- Nenasi (KL3U as the name I proposed – *'Keretapi Lintang 3 darjah Utara'*) and Mengkuang Valley in order to widening the Klang Valley which is very cramp and congested since last more than 20 years. I had 30 years living experience in Klang Valley from 1974 until 2004. The proposal[33] I wrote was dated 4 April, 2008. This is the map, key of the proposal

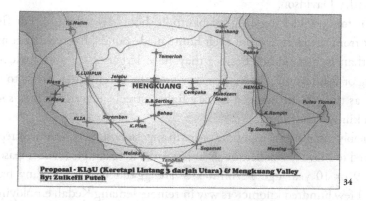

Proposal - KL3U (Keretapi Lintang 3 darjah Utara) & Mengkuang Valley
By: Zulkefli Puteh
34

Rural areas especially in the east coast like in Muadzam Shah or Pekan-Rompin looks quite. This is so because there are no social and economic activates there.

As it is now the villagers are traveling to cities to find employment as there is not much job in villages, even if there is any the wages they received does not substantiate to their effort.

Current social life standard with Astro, cozy fixtures, private transport and the demand for good education drives people to seek better job with better wages. Life isn't easy these days as most kitchen and household items carry higher price tag.

---

[33] Actually that is the first (series of 3 sets) copy (dated 4/4/2008) and I was sent from Kedah to Datuk Seri Najib somewhere in April 2008 as that times he still Deputy PM.
     Eventually it is just after that in 2009 'the God sent' me to Datuk Najib's parliamentary area, Pekan. It's great … I don't know why. After that follow by so many copy and so many ways including big file in 2009 personally hand-over to his strong right hand man in Pekan, Dato' Ishak Mohamad State Assemblyman and Exco (now Speaker)

[34] Both - ZP's documents; 2008; *'Warkah Untuk Datuk Najib'- KL3U*

Families are growing larger by the day. Many villages felt the economic pressure never before. They need support mechanism to create some sort of economic and social revolution as to speak in their areas.

The basic minimum industrial wage of RM 900 per month plus overtime and side benefits and other perk is regarded very attractive to them. That's part of the reason why youths moved to cities.

People in the villages live in family community for some reasons. They are comfortable with current life styles as they do not require Ray Ban sunglasses, or Dockers slacks, or Nike shoes. Many still drive 1980 Ford Escort, or Nissan Sunny. Honda Cub is very handy and cheap for quick ride to places. They do not need a Harley Davidson.

As for food, wild kangkong, or bamboo shoots are a luxury. For fish they either get from the river or from their home made ponds. Everything runs much cheaper than city standard, besides they have larger space area for cash crop gardening or fish farming, however many growing up children, prefer to work in big cities as they are influenced by city lights, streets advertisements, social life and such kinds of freedoms.

Inevitably cost plays an important factor in any establishment. Many entrepreneurs are tempted to move to smaller towns in Jengka as for example for cost reasons.

Last 9 or 10 year ago Permintex a Trengganu based company had their factory set few hundred kilometers way in remote Jeniang Kedah employing 6000 workers. Wages paid within the area if by policy minimum wage of RM 900 per month is lucrative enough for the villagers.

Such industries if set up in Muadzam or Rompin, both can expect to benefit from it. People do not have to hassle with heavy traffic to travel to cities to work. They save the daily motorcycle risks ride and cost. But with existing infrastructure, who will invest there.

It's the infrastructure that helps to shape the nation. My proposal Mengkuang Valley in the mid of Peninsular should be created to take over congested Klang Valley as KLIA (KL International Airport) at Sepang took over Subang Airport. An isolated village like that the property value will jumps up many folds later.

The authority should consider to have the necessary infrastructure like train track connecting cities to the new proposal sites. Such infrastructure would encourage industrialist to put their plants there. Industrialists point of view it so great to see train like this busy run in the country.

J006 - PERMISSION PENDING

UM 26/10/2010
The longest train – about 50 to 60 containers

35

One journey like this will take off 50 or 60 (lorry) prime mover and about 100 persons of night drivers (E class licence in Malaysia) besides lowering down the statistic of accident which is a big burden to the country right now.

The country also facing the lacks of these drivers (E-class licence) due to the authority only interested to train ALL to be racing drivers. Every Saturday night you will see the events throughout the country to proof the statement[36]

The authorities have the privilege to regulate policies which could encourage parties, entrepreneur and workers to benefits. Good policies and team understanding are necessary to enhance development.

The government must learn from past experiences of why companies moved away from here. It is very sentiment Bata shoes with its own record very long stay (maybe more than 50 years) in Klang had run out. Phillips in PJ had moved to Indonesia. P&G (Fab) to Vietnam.

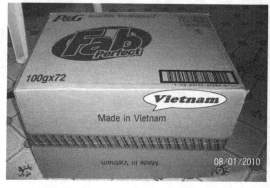
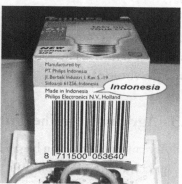

37

---

[35]   News, UM 26 Oct, 2010; KTM Longest Train
[36]   An illegal night racing on public road.
[37]   Both - ZP's Collection, 2010;Interest.

Many more companies will move to Vietnam or China. It is due to unsustainable policies besides cost. Why not they make the factories who need to move would be move still in the country as before for instance from KL (Jalan Bangsar) to Petaling Jaya and then to Shah Alam. One of the good places would be an author proposal, along railway track KL3U.

One of the most important things will happen drastically is 'KL region' will become wider. A lot of a middle class will run away from KL centre yet still work in KL.

New places for them would be Jelebu, 40 km; Mengkuang, 80 km; Cempaka, 120 km; even Muadzam, 160 km. If in Japan it took just one hour by train from Muadzam to KL. Then can use bicycle-train-bicycle to office. One hour can use to read newspaper. So that in evening.

What is the big impact? You just imagine KL life, very big difference. How much difference due to emerge of Putrajaya rather than still stay in KL.

Who really 'fit in' then only stay in KL. Middle class has choice not to stay in KL anymore. There will be less rushing and traffic jam during holiday. Actually a lot of problem would be created if cramp and congested.

Cool new township will attract development of condos, shopping centre, special activities like jungle call and recreational too. The most important is 'near' KL.

Kuala Lumpurian weekend can be as far as Nenasi (200 km) or straight to Tioman Island. They can just haversack, overnight or comeback on the same day. They can leave children confidently because of the short period and feel not far away.

On the other hand, you just imagine what will happen to Nenasi and its surrounding, accommodation, eating places, taxi, workshop, handicrafts, fishermen, farmers? How about Tioman Island? Ferry services and related will sense the virtue of changes.

3.3 - Agriculture – The Only Way

Agricultural revolution began in 19th century, during which new technologies in agricultural production were introduced to improve and increase crop productivity.

It was an agricultural transition period from relying heavily on human or animal labour and primitive tools to farm or cultivate agro-product and for further transition to more advanced productive methods resulting in the restructuring of social structures. This includes green technology research and development and technology transfer initiatives that increase agricultural production – precision Agriculture.

In this context, Malaysia has done so much to this industry no one can deny. The effort had improved management skills in agricultural production. Many small time farmers benefit from the effort. The question is how right is their direction?

As comparison, lets us overview at the industrial transition in Malaysia. Have we got the compass right?

Led by Dr. Mahathir (4th premier) started very well in shaping the industrial sectors within a reasonably short period of time since it came in some thirty years ago. Since then they had developed many industrial areas and brought in many foreign investments.

Their favourable policies had encouraged American, European and Japanese companies to put factory plants here. They provided to them special incentives and concessions such as pioneer status, grace period, tax holiday, duty free for imported machines, allowing expatriates in etc.; the impact was they created a robust socio-economy.

Thousands of jobs were created. Allied businesses grew alongside. Suddenly kaboom!!! Like an explosive, everything started to move. The cities were in motion. The street lights became merrier with advertisements. Shops full of branded products. People running on their toes busy as ever. Transport and logistics was whizzing the streets.

Telephone operators work round the clock tending to nonstop calls. There were laughter and sing along till late night. Cashiers counting cash collection was more often with security officer's eyes wide awake and hands trigger happy for possible intruders.

That was the impact of the industrial policies which restructured their socio-economy. All in all today we see they got the industrial directions right. Thumbs up!

However time has changed. The Ministers had changed too. The industrial and commercial sectors are taking a down turn. It will not be discussed in here.

In the agricultural sector we do not see similar busy activities. Things moved in at much slower pace. Palm Oil production like CPO (crude palm oil) and down products depends on very much on export at unattractive prices.

Many small holders were affected. Rubber too has declined its demand as synthetic rubber was taken as substitute. Moreover price has dropped so much to cripple the industry.

Many green vegetables and agro-crops are grown on higher land. They are dominated by the Chinese supported by the employed Banglas. The crops go as far as Singapore leaving the left over with in their market.

The agricultural green crops' market network belongs to the Chinese who controls practically all hypermarkets. The weekly street market which sells green crops and vegetables are dominated almost by Malays.

This type of market is popular among the people living in towns and outskirt of cities. The government has stepped up through it agencies to promote small farmers product. Nevertheless, this happen only in isolated areas.

We practically have various seasonal fruits in abundance like 'rambutans' J011[38] the hairy fruit or 'durian' the horny and thorny fruit, nevertheless most are just left to rot or waste or giving away to monkeys for fiesta.

It's a pity that many just don't know what to do with it. Even if a bi-product can produce from it, the cost, that is the transport take most of it. Factories only concentrate in industrial estates or places distance away. So these fruits if any are just sold as disposal rates as no one would tend to it.

Transports are not eager to collect these fruits as the loads will no return. It wouldn't cover their expenses. So they cannot go anywhere.

Off late we see more professional taking up agriculture seriously as most commercial sector is already saturated. So many people fights for a small cake. So much so Doctor (PhD) and Engineer and others started moving into agriculture. Even much earlier, let see this paper cutting it was in 1993[39] agriculture will be the last good choice faithfully waiting for.

J012 - PERMISSION PENDING

Mingguan Malaysia 8/8/1993
Alahai PhD – Now interesting on agriculture

Some started chicken farming, livestock, fish farming and other in green crops planting activities.

Life has been no good of late. Inflation is on the high. New taxes take its kill hitting everyone. The villagers are pressured earn more for the family. They do not having better option but to find ways to better develop their own property or farms around then.

---

38   ZP's, Aug 2009, Putat Kedah
39   News, Mingguan Malaysia 8 Aug 1993, *Alahai PhD'*

There is plenty of unused land plots left attended. They see these empty lands turn to bushes and infested with snakes, scorpions, wild boars and monkeys to dwell and breed. Villages still don't have the conscience or naive to understand the meaning of the usefulness of these lands now.

Anyhow they know all around the world then. There is the need to produce more agricultural products for human consumption. In 2009, Malaysia import RM1 billions of vegetable per month (paper cutting - a few pages below)

In Hong Kong, the Hongkees, for instance, are already planting crop and vegetable on house tops, balconies and on any vacant land within the area of their condos and apartment.

There were trial made to plant on roof top years ago here, but many mocked the idea, but today after seeing the Hongkees doing it, it arouse interest of Malay professional to do more in this industry.

Many Malays are just born with simple, just contented with what they are. Except in Mahathir era the authorities also are dancing to the villages tune. They should fine better formula to encourage the village folk to do more to improve their livelihood.

In this respects education can play vital role to change their mentality. Some Malays are lazy mule. Effort must be made to move the mule. If it needs a crane to move them, by all means do it.

How was the wall of China built? How was pyramid of Sphinx, Pharaohs and others Pharaohs built? It's by human sacrifices. Their subjects were made to work otherwise they will get whippings. So there stood the pyramid and the wall of China.

Whipping no more place today. Alternative must be found. If we cannot 'push', there probably 'pull'.

Early education is necessary. Constant and relentless trainings are needed. Incentives are given more to small farmers who plant domestic crops. Provide them with good grains, or good bred catfish. Finance and technical support is necessary. Provide them with short term loans. Motivation and physiological support are very important.

Good human relation between the authority and the farmers is vital. Technology helps to support in every industry. Small farmers must be trained to make good use of smart phone or tablets. There are many useful applications in it. The internet is not a luxury anymore.

Agricultural mechanization must come with approved road carrier (like commercial vehicles now) to support. It should have proper running cost (less tax rates) to 'pull' the change of the Malaysian landscape. It will enable these vehicles to wheeze the streets and villages more often.

The authority should develop villages to be self-sustained with businesses.

3.3.1 - COMPLIMENTARY – YAZID STORY

The following is a typical problem of a Malay intellectual who wishes to change the Malay economic land scape, unfortunately there was no mechanism to allow him to proceed. It's just like ploughing the field with an old buffalo in the 21st century.

Mr. Yazid did not regret to have to return to farming as that was the best option for him to earn an honest living. His consultant firm was not doing well. It's hard to sustain especially many like him were fighting over a handful of projects.

What could he expect, as one project site visit he could see over 100 contractors present. The strange thing was the one who secured the project happen to be the same company all year round.

Yazid is principled minded Muslim. He like anyone else knew well about bad practices in government procurement for contracts. Most good projects were taken by the 'Chief' and his cronies. Those around him got smaller share of the bite. People like him received only the spill over. That spill over usually was lucrative enough to stay around for a year. One thing that's worries him was the contact carries scary conditions.

Yazid had been trying hard to resist all the illegal practices. He would be in trauma if he got unusual offers. It was very difficult to remove this stigma, like inflated prices of materials, dubious invoices, falsified bills, provision for politic, kick-back, commission etc.

These were the reasons why Yazid decided to change profession. He made him minds to leave the city and stay in remote Rompin.

Yazid is an experienced engineer. He is smart like any other professionals. He too had experienced working with few engineering companies before.

He saw most employers, especially Malay employers, take advantage of employees. Many times he had to opt his own pocket money to settle with subcontractors or got cheated doing sub contract work for contractors. Even employers often cheat staffs. In Malaysian business good friend will become worse devil.

Yazid started clearing the bushes on the 4 acre of land plot 3 km off the village trunk road on hands and knees. No heavy machines were used.

Their parents and grandparents usually would get together to take turns to assist fellow farmers. They came with all kinds of working tools though primitive. They built dams, waterways, planting rice grains and harvesting in community spirit. Such culture had long gone.

In to-days context, farmers would expect the authority (Ministry of Agriculture) to help them in any ways possible to start work. That didn't happen.

Let see what the minister did. He just shouting and barking as ever. He himself remarked (actually for himself) about 'RM1 billion vegetable were import every month in July 2009.[41] Since then what he did? Yeah ... after 3 years (Sept 2012) he showers one plant in the pot for consume 1 Malaysia.[42] As what we know ... it is just for show or political propaganda. Next another 3 years sure he will talks the same thing again. It is now 2016. Is there anything happen since then?

The agricultural authority has its agencies spread out complete with tools and machines. The agro-training centres as for example have trainees which could be useful to help farmers. That is didn't happen neither. All these agencies work according to their whims and fancies. That's civil servants' attitude.

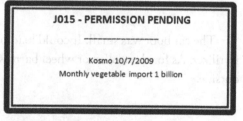

> **J015 - PERMISSION PENDING**
> _____
> Kosmo 10/7/2009
> Monthly vegetable import 1 billion

> **J016 - PERMISSION PENDING**
> _____
> The Star 28/9/2012
> Minister said no shortage of food here showing he watering plant pot

---

40 ZP's, Dec, 2010, Kuantan
41 News, Kosmo 10/7/09, RM1 billion
42 News, The Star, 28/9/2012, Food Shortage

Soon after bush clearance, Yazid started planting short term crops that is banana and in between planted various green vegetables and beans. Its real hard work though. There wasn't any machine used. He and his wife with high spirit ever started well in the beginning. His fate is rest in the hand of the Mighty. Soon after sometimes they got worn out. Yazid's faith shattered as they were stuck with various problems which he least expected.

Firstly his 30 year old Mitsubishi Gallant sedan was unsuitable for loading and unloading of tool and working gear. (See the picture – white car far behind)

The car boot was small. It could load only the most two bags of 20 kg weight fertilizer. As for the trolley or wheel barrow he stuffed in with half body hanging outside.

This was bad if driven on gazette roads.

---

43   ZP's, Dec 2010, Kuantan
44   ZP's, Nov 2014, Nenasi Pekan

It wouldn't be safe in the hands of police patrol officers. He would end up by getting tickets or squeezed for some money. Some policemen habitually perform their duty with bribery. Foreign workers, the Indonesian or the Banglas (Bangladeshi) irrespectively with or without legal documents were their piggy banks.

He realized it wasn't practical for him or anyone to walk to and fro from village trunk road 3 km in to the farm every day. Moreover there were tools and fertilizers too to be brought there. At times he engaged the Banglas to haul the fertilizer bags to farm site.

As for tools, he would load in the wheel barrows and walk them to farm site. It looked silly though compared with what he was doing in the city before.

He tried to codon himself from bragging irrelevant issues. He was really irritated. Many issues were disturbing him.

A pick-up would be convenient for him. He regretted for selling off his pick-up van while in the city. Most small time farmers couldn't afford a pick-up, or station wagon or any such kinds of transport as it would not pay back.

A new pick-up or a small lorry maybe is not expensive, but it is hell lot expensive after tax clearance and registration. Further for the authority charged exorbitant road tax and insurance for commercial vehicles. They carry up to 200% tax all in plus vehicle insurance and the extras. The annual road tax and insurance itself is about RM 3,000.00 or more and renewable annually. It means about RM 250 per month for rare and short drive on the road alone. It's absurd isn't it?

He is not in transport business; which most of the time using the gazette road. For this absurdity farmers resort to cheaper means of working transport (see picture – left, no.02)

It also 30 year old van.

Many used the fabricated wheeled carriers, or mini trailers or modified Honda Cub bikes complete with carriers or extra compartment etc. for lighter loads enough to bring things like fertilizers to farm site.

Isolated small time businessman or farmers activities are very much restricted as commercial vehicles do no service them because of the small volume of loads

---

46   ibid
47   ZP's, Oct 2010, Sijangkang Selangor
48   ZP's, Aug 2011, Sijangkang Selangor
49   Zp's, Sept 2013, Pekan, Pahang
50   Zp's, Aug 2011, Sijangkang Selangor

and short time usage of the road. If there are any, they would buy products at very cheap price to cover the transport cost and other overhead.

That why we can see the standard of Malaysian scenario; all commercial vehicles must be overload in order to survive. It's weird? Yes! Sure! Their ethic of works is no difference with gangster or robber, rob and kill.

They must do wrong thing and dangerous (to both parties) every day in order to survive. Let compare this. Both are same photograph.

,   51

C is sense for 'centre of gravity'. C1 (overloaded) very high due to high and widening top and just simply see the arrangement of the logs. C2 is (where it should be) very much lower more or less just like petroleum tanker.

Let see these photos Malaysian common practise

52 ,   53 .

If you plot an observation curve to study the dangerous behaviour it is really deviated and off-side to critical side forever.

We just imagine the stability and danger of this trailer. If suddenly something happen and a little shake of steering wheel, it would loss control and capsize easily. That is how danger this 'robbing' job. The wife is waiting anxiously.

---

51   ZP's, 2013, Endau Johore
52   ZP's;Oct, 2013, Pekan
53   Ibid

Actually with far sighted thinking, it is very heavy burden to the country and everybody due to very high counts of accidents. Moreover who has really related; especially one and family affected for whole life.

The short sighted Malay leaders cannot see that far. He only can see one dollar (revenue from road tax) which actually killing 100,000 dollars every day (should be generated by modern farmers and million dollars save by the road safety). Shameful Malay leaders just like 'their cows'[54] minded.

It is not surprising to see poor sight of business in villages. Farmers' activities in remote Rompin where Yazid lived die off. Many produce crops only for home consumption.

They are not be blamed for under development and they aren't stupid neither lazy. Is Malay leaders thinks all the 'pariah' Malay must be stupid and must be mule like this in order to make Malaysian high income? Are they eligible for their post?

55, 56

Talk about the money the people never stupid. They know how to calculate and decide to do or not. For stupid example; if that 'mule' can get paid 3,000 dollars per day by doing that job, or 5,000 dollars for this job [57] sure a lot of stupid 'mules' from Putrajaya will resign and chasing this mule job, isn't it? There is no mechanism to activate

---

54 Cows – Please see the cows and cross country in chapter 2 (part 6.4)
55 ZP's, Nov 2014, Nenasi Pekan
56 Ibid
57 ZP's, 1979, Putat Kedah

village development. The authority has neglected in their responsibility in village development.

The Malaysian envy to see the Arabs, Westerners and Europeans was enjoying tax free vehicles and other tax concessions. The Japanese, they too enjoy tax concessions.

They see those driving big limos and high powered cars. It's because they are cheap (relatively) to own one. They deserve it and that is law of nature, universal; not like Malaysian policies 'force' on peoples to buy decent car but the pocket just a coin. Apparently they should buy old lorry or pick-up, then work, work, work, work, work for their leader and GST.

How to enjoy those decent cars? Just the signal light broke by son's bicycle, no money to change it.

This car quite new but look like the hirer cannot pay the instalment. Now a day this is quite common. Without any down payment the car could be on the road. What for if you only can drive it for 2 or three months and one name is going bust? Beside that what the damage for the country? Do they deserve it?

Sure it is not like their former premier Dr Mahathir. In 1950's during his medical clinic in Alor Star he thrives and deserve for Pontiac Catalina plus driver. This is class of palace. He deserve since then and not suddenly yesterday.

One to remember that time the car is very rare. Alor Star the state capital of Kedah having maybe 2 digits of telephone number. Let see my card of his (Dr Mahathir) clinic, but off late (maybe 15 years later) in 1969.

---

58 ZP's, 2014, Pekan

Nombor Tertib 94 69

Bilangan Perasah _____

Nama _Che Zulkiffly b. Puteh_

MAHA KLINIK
12, Pekan Melayu, Alor Setar.
TEL: A. S. 846

[59]

It still shows just 3 digits of telephone number.

For the route to Kodiang (trunk road to north) in 1950's it's just one or two cars of Austin or Morris per day. It is inconceivable of Pontiac or Cadillac or Chevrolet Impala or Dodge and so on.

This vehicle, the pick-up, had never been farmers or business working culture like in the States, or Japan.

We see the American, Canadian, Mexican or Australian use pick-up and station wagon as family life culture.

This picture (in Sweden) was taken in September 2000 and not yesterday (2016).

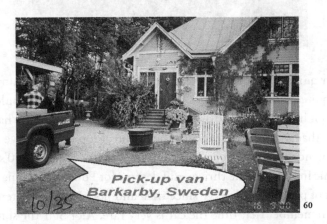

Pick-up van
Barkarby, Sweden

[60]

The Thais generally have the pick-up as life culture. It's weird to see the backward mentality of the Malaysian Authorities, or Malays especially. Their pre-conception of pick-up are exclusive vehicles for big project timers and the high up clans or sports.

---

59   ZP's, 1969, Clinic Card, Alor Star
60   ZP's, Sept 2000, Barkarby Sweden

The authority should encourage small time businessman and farmers to use pick-up for working convenience. There should be consideration to find solution to current unrealistic tax rates.

People say Arab has oil and their King is generous. So, most of the things come cheap. Malaysia has oil too but their Ali Baba Chief Minister is not generous. Nothing comes cheap. They let it be … because the 'Chief' is Malay. Malays are masters.

Everybody knows most of Ali Baba Ministers are, especially the Chief Ali Baba is sucking its citizen dry. 'Malay Supremacy' is his password to enable him and his fellow Ali Babas to plunder the nation. He uses all ATMs as his piggy bank, stole their savings.

Anything he does gets everything Okayed (ok). Why? It's for the take of Malay supremacy. No one can challenge him … not ever … consequences is you will be sent to Timbuktu.

Are you pretty sure that rightfully Muslim professes that? The word 'no' it mean as no! Yes, is mean yes! Everyone Malays in particular must be loyal to him. He is the supreme authority.

Yazid's was really frustrated to see the current state of confusion. The Malay authority which he upheld had not given him a dam!!! He was even frustrated looking at his progress. He felt weaker by the day. Questions after questions were bothering him. He knew it was bad to think bad about other people. Muslim thought him so.

A lot of professional like him, these days like to move to agricultural sector reason being opportunities in city has become saturated. Everyone knows that there are vast unused land plots either owned by the government or private individual. (These pictures were taken in Datuk Seri Najib parliamentary area – mainly like this).

These unused land plots could use for livestock, chicken or fish farming besides planting short term crops. But on second thought it's silly to change what is impossible.

Small time farmer like him have to work like a mule ... they depend on human labour more. What one would expect from Yazid who was in the late fifties.

The Thais their closest neighbours are smarter. They use all kinds of strange machines to help them on the farms. Most machines are either manufactured locally or fabricated at their home yard. This for example; long handle tiller. **J032**[62]

A small tiller strange like a stroller or 'baby walker' machine **J033**[63] is used for ploughing in place of the prototype one. It is cheaper than the small Japanese Kubota. At the same times just see the picture. **J034**[64]

How do you want to carry economical way these machines to farm site together with other necessary things?

The question is why can't their Ali Baba ministers think that far, to initiate in any manner to produce such **'reasonable running cost vehicle (buffalo)'** to carry the machines and products to anywhere by using gazette road.

These 'baby walker' is not practical at all to 'walk' with small wheel to the site of 5 or 10km away. It is sure there are many companies like Tan Chong (Datsun/Nissan icon in Malaysia), Inokom or DRB Hicom, maybe Perodua (who are strategically venture with Daihatsu) who are interested to do (build a very basic

61   All 4 - ZP's, Nov 20*15, Nenasi Pekan
62   ZP's, Oct 2009, Kelantan
63   ZP's, Jan 2015, Pekan
64   Ibid

pick-up van or small lorry) with the government protection policies. Why do they have to always be the consumers only? **J035**[65]

- Back to **'reasonable running cost vehicle (buffalo)'**, I do suggest
  - o Small lorry three tons and below and pick-up van have an option to register on private use like in Thailand and not necessary as 'commercial'.
  - o The road tax of 3 tons should be RM300 per year and RM100 for 1 ton[66]. Gradually reduce won't work. Blast it down then you can see the peoples like riot to chase an opportunity. Old lorries and pick-ups will be refurbish back. Workshop, hardware and spare-part will busy. Then you can see a lot of peoples drive 'working gear' to farm field rather than car. Surely less boys hanging around as their fathers need their help and it is implied passing their trade as well.
    - New style of recreation will emerge – their pick-up could carry scrambler to scrambling place even for picnic. That how they can utilize their leisure time. After school it is hardly these boys become 'National Liability'[67].
  - o The only major inspection (as chassis and body) for transfer ownership. Then second inspection (as a brake, tyres, light, wiper, paintwork etc.) for new owner. A lot of detail needed to be discussed. Only who in this line can give good idea. Don't pluck from the sky.
  - o After that they can fly on their own and bring back livelihood for their family and revenue to government.

---

[65] ZP's, July 2012, Putat Kedah

[66] Don't worry less in road-tax collection but you tremendously 'explode' income from 'uprising' agriculture which is currently tied hand back. It is win-win situation everywhere. It is more GST revenue without increasing the rate, less 'physical' gift and no more token cash (BR1M) as every citizen has their own cash like 1990's when they struggle for new share issue, new house, new Proton cars (even black-market). Visit Malaysia year 1990, Malacca's hotel full house, …etc.

[67] Please take note some graduate (some more in ICT, be able to write software/ programming) just selling (small scale) breakfast in the stall for more than 5 years, couldn't get a job.

Pekan, Pahang. 2016

68

- The photograph shows Toshiba fridge being transport. It is not near. Combination of primitive and modern (fridge).
- Are these two guys stupid? Of course no choice. The proper carrier is very expensive alternatively dispose[69] of is better.
- Let we think the 'hindrance' of our life in current context. Very easy way out – proper working tool needed. **'Then it runs by itself. Work with happy'.** The problem is the Malay government don't want Malay clan to live in modern life. They want to ensure primitive but the Malay clan persistently decline end up doing nothing wasting time. Nothing can do and nothing interested if you need to work like these two 'buffaloes'.

They have many technical colleges and training centres complete with robotic machines best in the world, unfortunately these colleges do not make good use of these machines to produce useful products.

Let see in chapter 2 - High Tea, Part 6.5 - Self Indulge R&D'.

Actually they do not have good trainers. Lecturers were typical civil servants. What can they expect? It silly isn't it. They have good machines yet they remain idle.

Most are for shows and for political propaganda to white wash public perception. They do not really see them work on something useful.

---

68   ZP's, Nov 2016, Pekan Pahang
69   To dispose of you still need pick-up to the right place. Otherwise it is another problem to environment and town council. Definitely it is no choice even if you view from any angle you like.

During the early stage production of national car, Proton, some like 1985 the former premier Dr Mahathir reminded; "Ford not only making a car, but Ford also selling a car."

It's very far and deep meaning for them to remember.

The Indians (India) students are far more advance in medical, science, physic, electronic or robotic. Where do Malay stand? At the end tips of the world.

Yazid said enough is enough. He had already worn out and feeling hopeless. Now he burying the hatchet gave up his agro-dream.

For him every aspect in agriculture was prepared by government but 'never launch'. The 'launch' means no reasonable vehicle to carry all that type of 'baby walkers' as 'trencher, 'peanut harvester' of course tiller and so on. In football, it means never attack. How to goal?

The Malay leaders are dreaming like drug addict under the bridge. They are forgot Malaysia is Malaysia.

Everywhere through-out the country is gazette road, not a cowboy country. You cannot crop just under your pants or in your skirts, must away from your house too. The pick-up or small lorry with reasonable price and running cost can do.

[70]

71 and 21 **72**.

Moreover this 'home made iron buffalo' at very low cost can join to the farm site by climbing this pick-up or lorry.

73

It's enough for help a farmers rather than walk to carry like this bunch of banana like Yazid does.

71   ZP's, June,2006, Jitra.

72   ZP's,2013, Pekan

73   All 4, ZP's, 2014, Pekan

Definitely we don't want like this condition of vehicles

to run on our road with high obligation to run their new emerge modern agricultural country. These no difference ethic and must be wrong doing all the times like robber or snatcher.

With that proper pick-up, it is not like a mule anymore. This scenario will automatically 'pull' young generation to agriculture. You just imagine without maximum full effort 'bull power' (of the manpower) to put in, come with scrambler and agriculture tools in that pick-up, tough hat-bare-chested proudly modern life style boys will attract the girls join in.

Surely it wills less vehicle on the road as new activities, 'scrambling' will emerge. Day time already tired as the money growing up in pocket. No more night racing. Follow by less in drug addiction.

They can independently plan for their own marriage. Ease for the family and ease for the country. All run simultaneously and automatically. Win-win for everybody and win for every angle. Moreover it sure to be needed some helper to do this and that in the farm.

---

74   ZP's, 2009, Jitra
75   ZP's,2006, Putat Kedah.

All these boys will be 'disturb' by elder brothers (modern farmers) for help and reward according to their time and effort. I would believe this kind of 'disturb' will be welcome by those boys with condition there must be a machine-assisted.

I would like to invites everybody to look Australian Peter Ryan and his family in their fodder factory where you can see how the machine assisted. (I am willing to adopt the photos but more times needed to get permission and maybe cost)

http://www.fodderfactory.com.au/gallery

Especially in Gallery image 20 of 30, you can see the pick-up carrying full load of fodder together with girl and children beside Peter Ryan. Image 19 of 30 you can see the lady and tractor at works.

Image 26 of 30 you can see the pick-up next to factory. If you could go through his website, you can find paper cutting (B&W) that show two girls hold the tray and fodder in factory during the Orange field days.

From there you can see it's doesn't matter whether ladies/girls or children like to join the parents who are 'modern farmers'.

Not like in Malaysia the farmers are the symbol of poverty and the symbol of stupid work (small return/reward – not even enough for phone prepaid) like mules.

It's must be changes.

… Yes! Machine-assisted and definitely not only a tool like a hoe or a cleaver.

It is cost too, The Malay leaders must understand to the fact of today life. The need of hand phone etc. is compulsory even for a poor farmer. It is on 'damage' side of your calculation which is pulling down your budget.

As they growth, they will get more experience, familiar and handy to work of course more 'reward' gain. For example, this boy but difference trade, workshop works (iron welding, electrical etc.)

---

76   ZP's,2015, Nenasi, Pahang.

77

He just 15 plus who help his father with small reward. He is getting skill better and better.

Whether he likes it or not at least he has a choice what to be. God willing all of these will help to resolve the Malay society problem which now is rotten to the core.

The future voracious 'disaster' is start some time ago. The Malay youths happy go lucky all the times round the clock and had no gut to control time wastage on hand phone and internet. The children grower and becomes full liability to the country.

It is very 'futuristic' for them to be outcast citizen and congratulation to the Chinese who had fully astride welcome by the Malay.

Since no fight for independent no bloodshed so as usual you just follow traditional way to take over this country. Racial riot like May 13, 1969 is not necessary at all.

Back to above if any boy cannot go further study to become a doctor, lawyer, engineer and lecturer and so on, instantly they can work (not likes apprentice)

---

77   All 4, ZP's, 2015, Nenasi

and immediately he could had some cash rather than stealing HT live working gear in substation[78].

The Malay authority cannot force against the nature, all driving learner must become racing driver. The stupid Malay authorities will sacrifice & concentrate to one of 1,000 victims, as what education does. They are blurring lost direction, lost actual target for the children.

The most important for children is they will be a good human being, good citizen and it's doesn't matter what their level is.

They (authority) cannot differentiate between 'learn' and 'educate' as their name of ministry still confuse till now.

The **'surface thinking'** they only think what the salary is and forget what the task are. That why sometimes due to misled become prostitute. At first is high class like one night is RM25k or virgin breaking maybe RM50k. After that it will very steep going down.

It's don't care how to get it, they thought all A's must be good. Finally examination paper as low as *'Ujian Penilaian Sekolah Rendah'* (UPSR - 12 years old children) leak by whom who supposed to take care?[79]

It's no differences with someone who concentrates on 2 children and forgets 8 more who tend to be drug addict. It weird and should be reciprocate, concentrate 999 of ordinary and commercial driver who will run the nation survival.

One cannot live with only proud and shouting all over the world (with nobody don't like to hear) of formula one winning award for the portion of calendar year if any. They simply don't know which more priority is either 1 or 999.

In actual life they cannot depend on magic. A good breed if drop in the sea become island. It's true according to the phrase but never happen. If drop, die! Mercedes, Volkswagen, Toyota even Proton (car) never emerge from 'Aladdin smoke'. The *'bomoh'* (native practitioner) still need to buy one.

What is the magic?

Suddenly just after the school then put down the pen straight become a farmer? Whole life never touch agriculture tool not, for example, like Peter Ryan family (Australian Fodder Factory).

Malay authority should stop dreaming there is no magic for real life survival. Everything should start from beginning or must be clever enough like their ex-premier Dr Mahathir to adapt on 'other people beginning' like Proton Car adapt on Mitsubishi, Modenas motorcycle on Kawasaki.

---

[78]   High Tea: TNB substation, Malacca
[79]   Please see in chapter 2 - High Tea: Lesson for the Education Ministry by Dorairaj.

Eagle Aircraft bought on the right time. Lotus Company was taken over with sincere (to owner too) with proper consideration not only buying one unit of Lotus car. {Please take note after win Lotus, Proton (Malaysia) was 'at par' with his bidding competitors giant car makers – only that time}.

To start from beginning Honda start with **50cc Cub** engine, not straight on 1000cc Goldwing. Notice it! Even 50 cc it is working tool (please see the goods carrier).

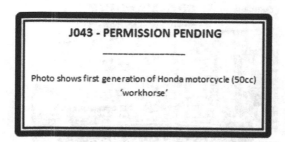

J043 - PERMISSION PENDING

————————

Photo shows first generation of Honda motorcycle (50cc) 'workhorse'

80

Meanwhile the readers can surf in internet.

It means get the small money first and gradually up. So in education; step by step and not like monkey play (all 4 legs grasp everything and choke up in the mouth) non-stop feeding bog down with school work in full scale confusing.

He (Yazid) was thinking wild to fabricate small farm machines instead or doing something else less problematic.

The Chinese in cities felt the pressure too. They felt the impact of poor economy and market performance.

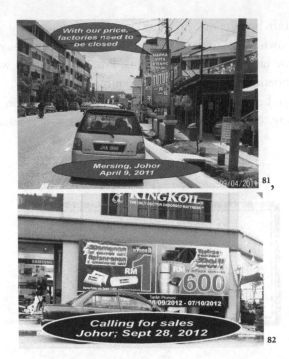

Nevertheless they have long hands. Moreover they get the support from their own clans, the association. They would migrate if necessary. Their ancestors had long history of migration, unlike the Malays; the idea of migration is rubbish.

They are thinking of their chicken or cows at home. The poor Malays could not think that far. So the only option is to open hands for government aid or, to return to village or jungles to live in isolation …

The real failure of UMNO government …

At the same time is my failure too who tick BN/UMNO, especially Datuk Seri Najib personally at Pekan P085 with the polling ticket serial number were 046600.

Somehow rather I never regret because I believe UMNO is not to be sentence and UMNO is not belong to any single Malay.

---

81   ZP's,2011, Mersing
82   ZP's,2012, Pasir Gudang

PART 4.0 - SOLUTION

4.1 - Religious

The solution for the Malay is only and the only is they must back to their religious[83]. Any other religious cannot accept the Malaysian Malay unless it is ready to be spoilt.

Do you think Japanese will accept the Malaysian Malay to join in and 'make changes' to their culture as what Malay does? Not even need too far just go to Singapore it is enough. Then we can see the difference between civilize and uncivilized.

The Malaysian Malay if they have to go to Singapore they would not simply throw rubbish. But in Malaysia, just after 'night market' you can make hilly rubbish[84]. I am so curious because I never simply throw anything even as small as sweet wrap

Even Malay Bruneian is very precious civic minded, full discipline on the road transport highway, courtesy like Swedish or any Europe country to pedestrian.

They must back to the real Islamic track which is too deviated and mislead. They should gather to new converted Chinese-Muslims and Indian converted especially. As what I see I really scared about my born Muslim compare to them some sort like the heaven and earth, not even part per million of them.

---

83   Religious here is universal talk. If more detail we need to refer to appropriate body. Then forward to 7.10 – Religious.

84   This is the real short-sighted cannot think a little bit far. Late my father and *'ustaz'* (Islamic scholar) since my childhood always remind firstly 'the God will see what are you doing' secondly 'what you get (by doing that such thing)? I don't think I am good, but it is an obligation – just for our own sake, the living world.
Furthermore it is incurred unnecessary heavy cost to answer to the God on our participation. Islamic faith said, The God will 'calculate' the good and the bad even how small as particle is. It is meaningful to keep sweet wrap in your pocket and throw in the right place. Then your 'Heaven tally counter' will add additional record. For non-Muslim, forget it, it is still good if Malay could throw rubbish in the right place. It is enough.

Malay born Muslim must realize if they don't want to be outcast[85]. Try to reinstate of their Islamic faith with comparing to converted-Muslim[86]. Then only we can see the differential and where we are.

Analogy: A good sea side born Malay never realize how good of his place because he used to it that his toilet also on the beach. His beach is pedestrian not like Kuala Lumpurian

So after as long as born-Muslim just gathering with the same gang since childhood, better see out of the box. Then you can see how small you are that your quality (Islamic) was too much faded.

That is very big scope. Let we narrow a little bit.

Main scope is back to Islamic faith. Please forward to 4.2 - Faith

Then narrow it to use brain power.

Everything we must think. Then please forward to 4.3 - Think Philosophy.

If we really know how to think for universal benefit and for the Day After (as Muslim faith) you not even have superbike or so many cars like Zaxxx Haxxxx[87] had.

Let we see this derivation of 'Thinking'. I would like to throw one of a lot of things I had from my observation of Chinese 'thinking culture'.

This is one of their exceptional 'positive thinking' compare to Malay, it is 'Principle and uphold'.

Before we move to that issue I would like to draw attention of overall first. After the 'religious' matter this is the key of any discussion for Malay survival. I am quoted Tun Daim Zainuddin (ex-Finance Minister); (Fatini, 1997, p. 124)

---

[85]   But for this 'species' (no pray species) nothing to worry at all because they can assimilate (subject to 'wicked' only) as anything in any culture. They can be warrior / commando to anybody except to their clan.

[86]   Islam is not belonging to Malay.

[87]   Zaxxx Haxxxx – I think about 30 over units all expensive one (as twelve years before in Country Height). All arrange in compound like high class used car centre. It is in my expectation it worth about 20 million easily. It is unconceivable the Islamic long loud utterance, vehement outcry just blatant radios. When you need that so many if you are really Islamic 'warrior'? Within short span of life where you want to go with all those cars? We are not curious if all over the country no poverty (relatively not so bad). Then he should ask back where all this money come from. In Islam there got simple question; "Would you get that such amount of money if you are not in that position?" or if gift, "Would the people give you if you not holding the post?" If any that is belong to the country and you must return – Islam taught like that isn't it?, unless you are infidel. Don't forget as Prophet Muhammad said "If Adam's son had two valley (full) of gold definitely he want a third one"

"Saya lebih suka orang Melayu membuat ketetapan, sama ada hendak berniaga atau berpolitik atau menjadi ahli professional. Jangan bubuh kaki atau tangan merata-rata tempat."

Malay should decide either

- business or
- politic or
- professional

Don't mix-up. (Don't put in 'your hand' or 'your feet' everywhere).

This is very simple and very easy to understand but you can create as long as you want no ending story.

Let me start;

Business + politic

- Minister busy with his own business (Nation become secondary)
  - o He will use all resources for his business
  - o He will channel any related to his ministerial or to his power to him or his wife end up super unrealistic prices to kill 'rakyat'
  - o PM Mahathir runs the nation at the same time he still runs his business medical clinic in Alor Star, how?

Business + professional

- Medical Centre & Specialist Doctors
  - Doctor don't care will finishes his task to save patient (professional), but it will not be happen if the patient had no money (by business / management)
  - So doctor in his position (professional) cannot manage medical center. Alternatively he must put aside his 'doctor'.
  - In construction, 'A' class contractor must have project engineer. The Malay contractor (business) as usual is super tremendous king of cheated sure he want to cheat the owner of project for extra *'haram'* (Islamic forbidden) money. But professional engineer will not to sign if let say the contractor only put 3 point of piles instead of 15 pcs in the specification.

Politic + professional

- Judges get in politic. Let discuss
- Attorney General get in politic
- Retired appeal court judge, once he against prime minister (look like he sided to opposition party), another time he against the party who want to charge prime minister because it is not constitute for certain section – Then he is real professional even retired
    o   If he is still in office, politic cannot influence him. He only sided to the 'rule of law', must comply.

4.1.1 - PRINCIPLE AND UPHOLD

4.1.1.1 - The son employ his own father.

This story is about 1980iest. Father works as company driver to his son. Beside that elder and younger brothers and sisters also work with him in chicken farm in Klang. He owned BMW 323i. That time it is rare and too elite.

One day, that BMW was sent to workshop (where I work - clandestine[88]) for servicing.

During servicing the driver (father) was grumble about his boss (his son), stingy, very calculative, cheap on salary even though drive expensive car, simply trample down into chicken feces it is never mind. Then really dirty with chicken feces undercarriage (inside is good)

One day the boss comes to take serviced car. He patted on my back, "come!, let test the car".

On testing, in third speed (maybe) he smash the dashboard, "Haa!! This is a car". Really high performance. I cannot feel the difference before and after service / high precision tuning even I did it (some sort I make racing car, other people only can feel the precision of performance) – just follow the rule and procedure isn't it? – the 'result' will accordingly.

---

[88]   It is in order to get precious experience – expensive car workshop (up to Jaguar and Bently and some of rotary engine). I act as the man with no scholar (but within short period the boss comes to know because I accidently speak English with customer. He cautious because he suspects I am police's 'special branch'). That time very hard to get job especially I am Malay to get in Chinese workshop and everywhere on the gate is stated 'No Vacancy'

It is rare in Klang for that time, our tuning is computer aided and the price of the computer system easily can buy two Toyota Corolla[89] (relatively now by comparison in tangible value is about RM 150,000)

Barely he spent for this servicing / tuning is about two thirdth (2/3) of the price to overhauling Toyota Corolla. Very expensive task.

I took opportunity to ask him about his father.

"Is that driver is your father? Why he always complaint and scold you stingy?"

"That's right! But he is driver. Must be driver's salary. But when Chinese New Year festival time, haa!......that time is father!. New Year recently I gave him RM20,000[90], 'from the son to the father'. But the bonus is driver's bonus, no father deal"

> **We must have principle in business. Don't agitate everything of non-business inside.**

4.2 - Faith

It is normal for everyone to support what he thinks right. It is prejudicial in most ways. Thinking is one thing but action often takes a different course. Hyper-smart people tend to manipulate his thought. Honest and God fearing people tend to rationalize his thought. Even religious imam could violence facts to fault or vice versa.

The Holy Prophet Mohammad peace be upon him has mandated that patriotism (love your nation) is part of Islamic faith. Islam not belong to any clans is a universal religion without boundaries and its teaching has profound wisdom and logic. In fact now a day we can see converted Muslim is very much better practices than original born Muslim especially Malaysian Malay.

The holy Quran stresses on the obedience to authority in the following verse:

"O ye, who believe, obey God and obey the Prophet and obey those in authority from among you."

The Prophet has also said:

"He who obeys me, obeys God, he who disobeys me disobeys God. He who disobeys the authority disobey me"

The rules of obedience to the authority and nation are clear.

---

[89] New Toyota Corolla that time is about RM14, 000 only

[90] New Toyota Corolla that time is about RM14, 000 only. That is how the value of his own father to this son. Somehow rather business is business and must be professional, then that RM20, 000 could come in reality.

Commandments in this regards are very practical and rational as to cut out the roots of rebellion and anarchy. Its philosophy is to allow Muslim to live peacefully. The doctrine allows utmost loyalty from Muslims.

As there are various nationalities and races, it is inconceivable and beyond logic to expect equal loyalties from everyone. Disloyalty to the authority would cause disorder and disrupt the harmony in the society. That the Islam though not likes disordered country who outcry claim as Islamic state. Today your turn (to kill leader) but tomorrow will be theirs and never ending.

Due to mislead and tremendously mishap The Malay leader should step down peacefully on the reverse route. He should gentleman for the sake of the country and he must realise his useless. That is the secret beauty of Islamic thought which is deviated everywhere.

It is inconceivable the Muslim need to kill each other as their Prophet Muhammad is so good even to Jews / non-Muslim who throw the shit on his head on the way to mosque. It's repeat every day until one day she fell sick. He pays a visit to her. Finally that Jews becomes Muslim. So where do they stand as Muslim warrior? Some more in Muslim thought in war (or any fight)

In the Malaysian context, the supreme authority is the royals, the reigning UMNO and its PM and the bunch of cabinet ministers and all the appointed officers who have authority. However if the nation ignores the fundamentals of the governing principles justice many will become fascist, intolerant and bigoted. The solution is to return to the teaching of Islam.

Muslim has effective antidote. It's the Quran, the ultimate solution. If ones minds are captive to prejudice, preconception or pre-judgment, one will never see the beauty or truth in Islam.

Firstly one must not have preconceived and negative notions about Islam. Many received or learned Islam from unauthentic and biased sources, so much so, many deviate away from the truth of its teaching. This great book of reference –has the message from Allah. It's a complete encyclopaedia for mankind on this planet earth.

Quran demonstrates the beauty, clarity and simplicity that are the clarity not only about the universe and its creation or spirituality and worship, more it is the clarity about the purpose of life here and after.

If one testifies that there is no God but Allah and testifies that Muhammad is the messenger of Allah, and then he or she must have total submission to abide to the rules as written in the Quran and with reference made to valid Hadith. He or she will never be deviated from the true teaching of Islam.

Islam thought us, amongst others, to exercise restraint, honest and helpful to mankind. One must be connected to Him every day, minutes and seconds. By doing so you will be protected from evil deeds and wrong doing. Allah will save us from aggression, occupations and exploitation.

Human beings face problems daily. Problem or whatever is within His wishes; therefore one cannot dispute the wish of Allah. Problem was born before human was born. It is Allah's will. Those who believed with heart rest in the remembrance to Allah, one will find tranquillity.

Islam promotes discipline and good behaviour, patient and self-restrained. It helps you to keep fit and healthy if you have good use of it, like fasting in Ramadan. Fasting is scientifically acknowledged as 'rubbish burner' as curative therapy. It is a good remedy for diseases. So think and ponder about it.

Human problems on this earth will be solved if you believe in Allah words. There is nothing impossible if ones have faith in Allah.

All of all those are their own (Malay Muslim) believe just on the surface, for show off and never practise properly. Where the Holy Spirit as is shouted? Just troublesome, they exploited and ride on Islam on the wrong manner until the whole world stamped to Islam is like now.

How about for non-Muslim, for instance the Japanese. After tremendously big disaster very valuable things (like gold) no loss and nobody claim as it is not theirs. That is the Islamic thought. Is the Muslim of Malay does? Where do they stand?

If a lorry capsizes, sometime in front of the driver there a lot of Malays like vultures rush for carcass and seize the goods. Why no shame and relentless? Muslim?

4.3 - Think Philosophy

The chocking and often confusing conditions of the Malays are merely caused by their traditions, cultures and social factors. These are just tips of the iceberg. Actually there are much more reasons which many of us know. However, the younger generation had brought drastic changes in their thinking mentality since the introduction of English education and its culture.

Professor Ungku Aziz, renowned Malay elite, is a thinker and philosopher (as to my opinion) is an icon in Malaysian economy. It was this man who introduced the cooperative systems and ideas, concepts now used successfully in the country. He was the one who established the Pilgrimage Fund Board- 'Lembaga Urusan Tabung Haji' (LUTH).

Previously pilgrims' activities were done by some smart 'Mamaks' (Indian Muslim) or individuals or religious heads many from the northern states and

Penang plainly for the sea port that connects Jeddah en-route inland towards Mecca or Medina.(that time there were no planes flying.) Today LUTH's success is known worldwide. Now the collection of deposits is in its billions. This is the result of 'smart thinking' introduced by this Prof.

Today LUTH, besides servicing its members for pilgrimage, it had spread its wings venturing in various businesses. It is a national achievement no one can deny. Currently LUTH has ventured in property development, construction, plantation (palm oil) and tourism (hotel) locally and abroad.

It's a product of this 'Prof. Think' that strikes gold. The idea was brilliant. With further wise 'thinking' and more 'creative thinking' the results are awesome. LUTH had turned a giant corporate entity now exploring mega businesses as it has huge funds. One couldn't imagine how much is its assets today.

Thanks to this great Prof. Smart thinking. He created a formula of simple conversion of deposits to the accumulation of funds and from there on garner businesses, without depreciating the unit value of the deposits, further, depositors earn and share the profit from the investments.

Today, more and more deposits are pouring in making LUTH the largest fund raiser in the country. It has its own building where members can be proud off. That is very deep/top secret and the beauty of Islam for Malay that they never realise.

They are just half boiled or half cook in Islamic practice[91]. Never think – the outcry of Professor may be. At glance is wasting money to go to Mecca but on the other side it is a great creator for calling a huge saving fund indirectly (if you might think). It's hard to call small 'investors' to open an account as low as 10 dollars.

Just because of their God it could. Everybody will involve and it doesn't matter from what level you are. That is a collective and that is 'small thing – big scale' economics. Today life and the day after are not apart. Malay never realises and always thinks separately. Those are their faith themselves. They are only used to direct feeding.

Tun Mahathir's (ex PM) brain child- trust fund, *'Amanah Saham Nasional'* (ASN) is another example of the result of 'think'. It seemed impossible in the beginning however today it has mobilized the fund raising scheme nationwide. Small and large sum of cash are pouring in. the ideas have brought more trust funds agencies, like ASB, Johore Trust funds etc.

One striking point to note here is indeed that this 'Prof. Think' really is a smart guy. His vision through 'think' culture *'fikir'* presented in many of

---

91   Let see chapter 2 - High Tea: the cows & cross country

his public forums title *'pembelajaran sepanjang hayat'* education for lifetime to encourage everyone to use ones intellectuality to 'think.' **J009(new)-tag**[92]

This is one of his speeches was invited by *'Badan Pencegah Rasuah'* (BPR = Anti-Corruption Agency)

He introduced this 'think' philosophy and gave its merit through his talks and in TV some 8-9 years ago. He remarked that many universities in this world gave less emphasis to creative 'thinking.' To him 'think' is the solution to many things, a way of salvation.

Many new things will come by if one can 'think' creatively and appropriately. In this aspect the Chinese can be given the credit. They are renown in these 'think' sorts of thing. They are ahead in many ways. The Malay has to accept the facts that they are very behind in creativity.

Obviously 'think' has brought tremendous development to human lives on this planet earth. It is a tool to enhancement of the quality of life. It had resulted in new living dimension. Many now are exploring into new ideas in development of business, politics and economy. Rubbish now (as seen with the sprouting of so many junk shops) as for example, has turned to useable products. It has transformed into big business. Many turned tycoons – rubbish tycoons.

One should ponder on this philosophy. 'Think' is a big word. It is the driver to human well beings like the driver to our computer. By 'think' or 'smart thinking' man develops creativity. For example: to cross a river, a traveller can cut short the travelling time by crossing by raft or boat. Further be makes the oars for peddling and for safety he uses various gadgets like ropes or cables to ease the task necessarily to cross with ease.

Or think further. We would build mega bridges and so on. Then there will be the element of cost to build the bridge and other consideration and so on. So are in the other fields of industries. There is this requirement to 'think' creatively in order to substantiate the investment.

In critical cases, however, like corruptions as for example, it would need 'clear thinking' necessary to substantiate the consequences and moral values of the person and country.

Many (Malays) claim to be Muslim. Soon after securing power then the devil – 'greet' comes in. The interpretation 'moderate' Muslims is the excuse for legitimizing kick back, bribes, abuse of power and authority. There is this wild

---

[92]   Extract of BPR activities public acknowledgement booklet.

imagination to getting quick cash through illegal means. These devils are prepared to sell away their dignity to the dogs.

Finally Malay should turn back to their religious or gradually to be outcast.

4.4 - Restructure; Education System and School Syllabus

When you start thinking it is good, don't over thinking.

Now all top clever man in education should try to think in reality, on the actual ground. It is must be proportionate with what we are. If we are about average of two meter high, don't ever think and make a plan in situation where we are five meter high. If we are 24hours per day, just think within.

Schooling time is time to learn and not time to glance through (due to many subject to cover) or time to revision

How the learning process?

❖ Let say Islamic Study, you need to teach them to become Muslim with strong foundation. As you create 'will power' inside them then they can find more on their own. You cannot cover all.

    o   If you bogged down you cheat yourself

❖ Let say driving school, you need to teach basic thing as the experience they can draw on their own later. Should you learn driving for 12 years as what Malay children learn English?

❖ Let say you want to teach someone become robber you no need to cover all and go to each target with them.

• Don't ever greedy,
• Don't ever be happy with *'Sistem Gila Syok Sendiri'*[93].
• Now the system is *'Sistem Gila'*. It is unrealistic over load.
• No time at all, the parent needed their children also!
    o   To clean toilet, room, fridge and so on[94].
    o   Customise their belonging.
        ■   Study table must be like table, and then if they work in office they will be lovely employee. Learn from now not in sudden to look awkward.
    o   To clean inside and outside of the house.

---

93   *'Gila'* = Mad; demented, insane, mental sick. *'Syok Sendiri'* = Self-gratify, self-indulge
94   Last time the students need to clean

- Learn to love clean environment.
- o They must know and use to wash their own underwear.
- o They must be cooking even for the boy. The needy of today.

- The children must learn how to become good citizen from their parent – time needed.
- They must have time to do something sweating.
- They MUST not obese – time needed.
- They must have time to talk to their parent then they know who their parent is.
- They must help the parent.
  - o That is standard Islamic culture and Chinese.
  - o Then the parent can pass their trade down.
    - Not all can become highly professional.

- The system must lesser than now especially in variety.
  - o If 30 channel TV series; what conclusion you have? Not even one you get.
  - o Let say 8 hours session – every subject 10 minute, for what?
    - It is better less for you get something.
    - You cannot cover everything in this life.
    - If full throttle every day – in spite cannot catch up – 32 subjects.
    - You happy to cheat yourself to look session is over but the return is zero.
    - Malay is simply happy to see unnecessary busy. Falsehood!

- Longer time per subject then more focus and concentrate with more / enough time, ample and redundant time. The number of subject should be less per day.
  - o Ample time – Last time the teachers teach and wait intermittently to let the student understand. It means give time not like on the run or rushing.
  - o This is example for 'concentration', 'focus' and result;
    - Now a day I use computer to design and draw (for example in 6.5.3.1 – Paddy Industries)
    - Late 2008 I am able to design and drafting by computer (no more using graph-paper) after 2 days x 9 hours learning time. I'm very lucky to get one to one teaching style by just clever

teenager boy who knows to cover up all important aspects and sample in one go. Finally he said, whatever I teach you within two continuous days, we had to learn in two semesters (about one year) in polytechnic.

- The issue here is I can concentrate, focus then I got 'one' – at least something (and so useful until now - utilization) rather than 32 subject in one go end up nothing. After that get the other thing.

- Due to longer period per subject will need not the teacher come full time full day a week
  o Plan to be alternately like lecturer then they have time to correct paper at home or to adjust their own need with other authority which their time keeping were same.
  o Like now they need to sacrifice their night family time. In fact at the school they cannot do even doing nothing.
  o Save petrol, energy, wear and tear and green effect
  o Maximise each day time at school
  o Now the right time and no more fuddy-duddies

- Students too relax but high useful knowledge is more, which one better?

Ample time, 'focus and concentrate'

- I had experience 12 years since childhood learn English but cannot speak.
  o After that just about two or three weeks in international company I already be able and consider fluent in English
    - It is really big surprise of my Chinese friend when I spoke English with him. So many questions arouse.
  o Another story of English class if I not mistaken 'CML' in Shah Alam my friend with a lot of his friends took about one month to be fluent in proper English conversation and syntax. Before that he never speaks.

There we just imagine what the impact of 'focus and concentrate' rather than 12 years learning[95]

---

[95] In midst of 1970iest the teachers from America (Peace Corp) need to learn Malay language only in six months. After that they will teach in science subjects such as

That shows the Malay authorities mainly are useless and very stupid[96], mislead and don't know where they are going to. Whole clan is going to be outcast soon due to today world challenging life and their 'sleeping and lengthy' happy go lucky for ever.

Holiday is holiday (Is there any holiday is not holiday?). That the very basic word 'holiday' the Malaysian authorities not understand. That how they manage the countries? If the man we consider 'the man without principle'

In the last one and half decade, there are try to 'change' the 'guarantor' is not guarantor.

Then we can imagine how bad they are. How is the litigation to work through?

Recently August 2016 there were the issue of Syariah court case;

So many headline displays

'When statutory rape doesn't really mean statutory rape',.......Man on rape charge escapes jail after marrying victim, 14,.....Shouldn't statutory rape mean statutory rape?

4.5 - Restructure on Everything

Finally Malay must know how to use brain to think in order to keep the whole clans in the real-life environment.

4.5.1 - THEIR RELIGOUS

They must adhere in their mind all the time with Islamic faith where all over the world of developed countries practise it successfully[97]: -

"The good wise man in Islam is who is useful to society"

This mean make easier for the people. This is common life in civilized countries but the Malay authorities is 'jihad' (working hard) toward uncivilized and to become pariah[98] country.

---

physic or mathematic in full Malay. They did it successfully
[96] Sorry for the perfected word usage.
[97] They are not practising but they did as what Islamic taught then the Malay Muslim try to show smart by contradict with. The God will give as what you request for. If you adopt of weed killer 'recipe' you will get weed killer and so with if you adopt a chicken rice recipe you will get the right thing.
[98] Pariah – this word will belong to Malay and no more Indian as they are on civilization.

It is a lot of bureaucrats who involve in planning are real wickedness and useless. It is inversely to the real significant Islamic taught, they will work furiously to give troublesome to people and to spoilt the Malay management and the Malay clans as a whole.

4.5.2 - DREADED SAVAK

If we are concern on 'the Malay crafted artificial Islamic management' itself for example 'Pre-marriage Course' now become 'dreaded Savak'[99] (Roose, 1997, p. 388) of Shah Iran.

As what I said they only thinking how to be cruel, ruthless, tyrannical make the people suffer, horrific, terrible, miserable, dreadful, mishap and whatever bad wicked thing in this world are theirs. It is for what?

That is just to show off how power they are because they don't have any good thing to show like Professor Ungku Aziz (in 4.3 - Think Philosophy).

As a result of that experience now Islamic youth 'leaving Islam' (no more believe Islam is good) to the 'wild life' and become 'freedom' as they escape from big disaster and wild carnivorous kingdom.

From easy and short word '*baru*' they change to more longer and problem '*baharu*'.

From good size of <u>coins</u> for easy differentiates they make whole 'havoc' throughout the country by making almost same size. Every time one must look so many times to ensure it is correct – spend too much time for the super stupid small value (a few cents). Not like civilised Japan they had 'pokayoke' or Britain that they have 'British Standard' to expedite the value of time and the essence of life. All these were comply to their Prophet Muhammad and Quran {103 Al-Ashr (it mean 'Time');1-3} but they are not practising. They learned particles count for the good and bad will be accounted for Hell or Heaven – no escape!

4.5.3 - DATABASE

If they make <u>database</u> let say for school, it is so huge to useless. Since the father's income-tax file number also include plus so many thing to show extremely stupid they are. It is proven due annoyance to the schools and parents and the useless of that database. Nobody likes to use it. It is 100% non-user friendly.

---

[99]   The Shah's Iran secret police.

Aftermath they earn their salary for what? Is it the confetti of Hellfire? Pay must benefit / not to baton to paymaster, otherwise resign!

It should be proportionate and accordingly to the usage. If any software required they will ask the highest top in the world end up not even part per million they can use it. Normally it is hard to use it due to complexity. Analogies they only need 3 seater aircraft but they ask for Airbus 300 with full facilitate. As the result it is worse or maybe totally useless because one is the pilot problem and another thing nearby airport only can support small aircraft

How much lose to tax-payers due to paying their salary and a lot of hassle things created for nothing like paper, electricity, correspondence, at site staffs' salaries to entertain their 'rubbish' and so many things incurred.

Whoever endurance in private sectors obviously notice Malay bureaucrat is too much superfluous not even 20% effectiveness. It is very high burden to the country right now. Wait till the Day After, the God will tell you which calculation would up to mass of 'particle'.

Figuratively private sector, the man is at 70kg but in Malay bureaucrat corpulent look to 350kg. Just imagine, could you? Whether you agree or not the fact is reality.

4.5.4 - SHORT COURSE

Another area of concern there are some academic colleges it is too small I have seen much more effective. These under certain government bodies but look like 'clandestine'. Not much publicity and a lot of people don't know[100]. Their way is 'straight to the point with highest quality'. That is under labour/human resources ministerial. This particular concern is situated in Pekan

I have seen quite close experience where the girl just after school certificate joins in for two months (only), then four months industrial training also in Pekan.

Two month classes (I had to borrow to see) are good compact syllabus and applied. Normal in education system it takes four or six semesters. Why so long? Yes it was too lengthy – 'too much talk doing nothing[101]'. If about office equipment (office assistant course) alone we can elongate until one year if we like. Another

---

[100] Maybe they act as low profile style in order to avoid a pillory to education ministerial which look like so useless and extremely wastages.

[101] It means so many non-relevant to the core subjects (the purpose is to fail the student to show great). So many things you want to put in like monkey play.

year is just about how to open a file so we can make the course till 5 years[102] with no problem.

The beauty of that girl is she had been offered (with strongly recommended by staff surrounding her) by that company itself to be employed after completed her course and a few various companies (some associated company and vendors) including Singapore. Then she confuses which one she should take rather than others with 'lengthy course' interview by interview never get.

4.5.5 - MILLION DILEMMA AGAINST BILLION

```
┌─────────────────────────────────────┐
│ ┌─────────────────────────────────┐ │
│ │     J300 - PERMISSION PENDING   │ │
│ │     ─────────────────────       │ │
│ │                                 │ │
│ │     Utusan Malaysia 29/10/2008  │ │
│ │  Khalid defence his standing on appointment │ │
│ │           GM of PKNS            │ │
│ └─────────────────────────────────┘ │
└─────────────────────────────────────┘
```

                                                               103

Just to think how severe the corruption level and misconduct by Malays if they hold any post.

This not solely matter of talk it is quiet common on Malay practices

Ex Menteri Besar (Chief Minister) of Selangor Tan Sri Khalid defence his standing on appointment - October 2008.

'..........between loss of a few billion dollars in the hand of Malay and earning few million in non-Malay hand'

---

[102]   There I heard pilgrim course to Mecca about one year make confuse/chaotic as the good course is about two week only. That shows if too much feeding land out rubbish. That what happen in Malay education

[103]   News, Utusan Malaysia; Oct 29, 2008

PART 5.0 - THE CURRENT SITUATION

Currently the middle class and lower were facing crucial financing time. Day by day it becomes worse. Government pawn-shop not enough cash to finance large sum anymore. Some prominent banks had to close some branches i.e. CIMB which related to Malay especially already close 23 branches. Then the Maybank following some.

The disappointing thing is in spite of that 100.00% 'disaster' cause by Malay leaders, they never admits and like to turn the reality to upside down. Otherwise a lot of correction can be done.

5.1 - The Proud of Failure Party (UMNO)

Perpetually proud but failure is quite big problem. In fact "The Malays have apparently learnt nothing from the near loss of their country in the past" -----Tun Dr. Mahathir Mohamad: The New Malay Dilemma - JANUARY 24, 2008 BY DINOBEANO.

The Malay leaders are not clever enough just take it easy as they never show they are more concern especially on 'invisible' actual need of citizen. They like to forget and threat whatever small 'particle' is no danger. They vanish out of their memory the catastrophe on UMNO in last 28 years rather than learn something indirectly.

Judge Harun Hashim's findings that UMNO was an illegal organisation on February 4, 1988.

Let see how 'small dangerous thing works'.

UMNO an illegal organisation
The matter is small but when it starts like a match to burn entirely.
Encik Azizi Shariff (branch chief of Jalan Hj Hussein KL) very aggressive shouting, crying even he is as bottom level chief. UMNO high ranking feel like nothing going to be happen. They feel permanently proud, perpetually immune to litigation as they are government, power!

They prone to hit first and then looking for someone (power) to cover their misdeed. The issue look small but it perfectly sharp unavoidable head on collision. Encik Azizi is not a lawyer but he can see how severe and danger is waiting. Nine branches of 46 in Titiwangsa division were not register with registrar. There for the meeting were not valid and cannot send representation. But the most important is an offence since unknown date.

Section 12(3) Organisation Act was stated[104];

If any registered organisation establish any branch without permission of registrar, the organisation and that branch is consider as illegal organisation.

How big UMNO and how small this sentence?

5.2 - About Suggestion

You can suggest[105] anything but the mule is a mule. It is real hopeless.

They should look into planet where they are and make their contribution known – without looking like a braggart like Mahathir does.

There are a lot of thing to think of by their advisers or helpers.

For them to hire people they feel comfortable with isn't what they needs. They should look for people who can do the job best, even if he doesn't get along[106],[107].

They should learn why Mahathir brought 'outside' Daim as Economic Adviser and Finance Minister 'in' and what the result is?

It is no need to be highly educated to understand this; 'When you're climbing Mount Everest, who you choose as a partner can make the difference between success and failure'.[108] If you win, the winner is you and so if you are failing.

How, the Malay leaders?

---

104   This is not professional law translation. Please consider to the basic idea of content.
105   For examples, under Part 3-Commerce Malaysia Perspective and 6.5.3 – UMP.
106   Somehow rather his goal must for the sake of *rakyat* (citizen) and not plundering of the country.
107   (D.A.Benton, 1999, p. 409)
108   (D.A.Benton, 1999, p. 400)

5.2.1 - GLOBAL COMPETITIVENESS

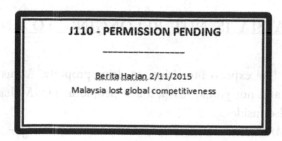

J110 - PERMISSION PENDING

Berita Harian 2/11/2015
Malaysia lost global competitiveness

[109]

This paper cutting shows Malaysia already lose global competitiveness.

Technology for production cannot anticipate the increasing of 'unbalance/ unparalleled' labour cost.

Whether we agree or not the main problem is uncontrollable inflation[110] was created since by the Prime Minister Abdullah Badawi in order to influence bureaucrat votes. Another big thing was 'prankish' with fuel price. He thought that dynamite he is playing is micro-mini fire crackers.

As what I said, this is full of politeness.

With this article it is enough for prime minister to make hundreds of move to overcome the current economic problem. The master key is there – Abdullah's 'manually inflated' is unparalleled to productivity should be overcome drastically. Then settled!

Instantly Malaysian labour costs become extremely unparalleled high. It was our weapon before. On top against economic principle, instead of reducing that was inflated in bureaucrat size to enlarge liability. Then proud! It is Malay leader mentality since British colonialism. Occupation is the only government servant.

I believe the writer is not an ordinary person. He Dr Zulkiply Omar must be PhD in economic. He is senior researcher in Malaysia Institute of Economic Research (MIER).

I as a layman still can see the article shows very worthwhile.

So the Malay leaders have everything to choose. It supposes not to be like now. Only stupid dump cannot see this good.

---

[109] News, BH 2 Nov, 2015 – *'Hilang daya saing peringkat global'*
[110] Inflation – please refer to chapter 3; 7.2 - Inflation

5.3 - Thinking Session

To all the Malay leaders and who going to be a leader;

5.3.1 - MALAYSIA IS NOT BELONGING TO ANY SINGLE LEADER.

i. You just like express bus driver to drive properly. A bus consider as a country and not yours. It is a lot of people inside. Mahathir as citizen now is also inside.

    *i. Dr Mahathir 'handover the bus' plus some cash for Abdullah with contented mind and unruffled spirit to continue good driving: "**UMNO can make a statement about the money I gave to Dato Abdullah when I stepped down. Better still Dato Abdullah can explain how much of the 1.4 billion Ringgit in cash, shares and property that my staff and one of his Ministers handed over to him is still with him**[111]". **During Abdullah tenancy.***

    ii. If you drive like drunk of cheap toddy[112] surely Mahathir and a few others cannot treat like nothing happen. Once you hit a rail guard, the whole bus unstable[113]; then you climb-up divider almost capsize like off-road adventure. After that straight drove in rubber estate, lucky not hit any rubber tree only small bushes and branches on top – no more side mirrors. By the time a lot of peoples realise, the bus should not be driven like this. Then who knows will come down to see the bus. Very bad since Mahathir hand over to Abdullah is not like this bad. It was broken everywhere like cross country.

---

[111] All finish? It is for Symphony Putrajaya la, shouting here and there fiestas, for son in law and grand incompetent (businessmen) cronies. Mahathir is sincere to let successor easy life handling the country for more flourishingly and successful. In fact Abdullah, Rais Yatim, Syed Hamid are from team B (against him – he took back to his cabinet). That is how nobleman is always trust the people with his principle, 'The winner is not winning all and the loser is not losing all'. Finally betrayed and 'back stabbed' by that exact particular trusted traitor. The country is going to grave red line. The analogy is the father handover happily his wealthy (1.4billion cash ++) to his son to continue prosper life but he fully enjoy dilapidating. But the father is still alive to see everything.

[112] Cheap toddy - a coconut-brewed alcoholic beverage

[113] The people who asleep still continue their sleep, full confidence the bus still comfort. But like Mahathir, ex-driver before feel difference.

iii. Then some peoples start talking to change the driver let he drunk himself. Whatever had is like that, what to do. The most important now is he supposes not to continue his driving anymore. It is a lot of people inside to consider.

iv. That analogy how were to speak.

ii. If Abdullah Badawi (the fifth PM) and Datuk Najib (current PM) were consider my suggestion (agriculture and precision agriculture) earlier, **Malaysia will be very busy now** no time at all for childish politicking (like Mahathir time in early 1990's – meeting can be taken at late night and midnight as no time at all. Highway can has hotel to support to minimise time). Busy and business totally upside down rather than now; not enough land plots like Lee Kuan Yew not enough land to inflate. Datuk Najib maybe not like now because most of people especially opposition also had a lot of thing to do. No time to peer over him. Psychologist said you (teacher) need to provide certain thing to do before you leave a class for time being. Just common sense isn't it?

iii. Everything will be negative;

i. If you create a lot of enemy for every second;

ii. If you think how to torture 'rakyat' most – A lot of 'created' heighten reinforcement matter to 'suck a blood'[114] - Town council parking, midnight very clear everywhere, least traffic you need nocturnal officer to summon 'tyre touch the line – not proper inside parking lot'?

iii. If you fight with 'rakyat' (citizen), inflation, GST, SPAD etc. You inflate bureaucrat size day by day to cater your problem and to 'suck rakyats blood' which already almost dry

iv. I never know Mahathir had bodyguard during his tenancy. Never see. Even somebody unintentionally met him (still as PM) in Sogo Mall is no bodyguard. Then after that the guy saw him to drive himself on small Pajero (Sport Pajero) still no bodyguard. So what the problem of you like flies flocking full of bodyguard and sometimes not even see your face. How much public money to spend for such protection?

v. Now you become formidable adversary to most of 'rakyat' except your arse-licker.

vi. When 'rakyat' going to throw a tantrum, they are not fighting like other countries to throw bombs here and there. They reserve and keep for just 'double crosses' - on Election Day. That how good

---

[114] How much can get for unfair bill to cover billion dollars of stupid debt.

Malaysian is. 'National riot' they already had and try once. It is enough for test and taste probably. Anyway 'Barisan Nasional' will get the whole 'profit of your investment' and UMNO to be sentence.

iv. Dr M on front line as warrior, *'rakyat'* were behind him facing the 'national' problem; he not fighting with *'rakyat'*. 'No time' said Lim Kheng Yaik. *'Rakyat'* feel safe behind him.

    i. Standardize Malaysian Time to become faster half an hour for West Malaysia; look east, IMF and Camdessus, Paul Keating and Australia, Margarette Thatcher and Britain[115], George Soros and financial crisis,

    ii. Venture Proton with Mitsubishi then Perodua with Daihatsu then buy and help Lotus, TVR, Modenas with Kawasaki, Penang Bridge – 'make and sell' and get money back plus profit to government; North-South Highway;

    iii. MSC (Multimedia Super Corridor)[116],[117] – Wall Street Journal hails as 'East Silicon Valley',

    iv. KLIA, Petronas Twin Tower, KL Tower, Cyberjaya, Technology Park, Putrajaya (not Mahathirjaya or Hasmahjaya or Mukrizjaya, not even one of Mahathir name?), Measat (satellite), rail transport

    v. Bureacrat time keeping, clock card, one stop bill payment. He instructs to speed-up a process[118]. Then Malaysia 'unleashes the power'. The foreigners coming for non-stop.

    vi. Tanjung Pelepas Port. Then Maersk and Evergreen gallop in from Singapore. Never mind next Singapore will swallow Malaysia. Gelang Patah already starts by Lim Kit Siang isn't it? Penang is already in the belt by his son Lim Guan Eng. If Malacca involve (Chen Man

---

[115]   Inflate of study fees and Tin Trade

[116]   MSC is Multimedia Super Corridor– Architectural by Mahathir. Who had attending on the International Advisory Panel Council Meeting? Who chairs the meeting and where the venue is? Please forward to
7.6 – MSC and Califonria

[117]   750 square km (50km x 15km) with main 'spinal cord' of 2.5 – 10Gbps and second level fibre optic at 622 Mbps were impress to investors especially on high-tech and audio visual who need broad band-width.

[118]   For example on Rafidah; Hotel developments' licenses from 62 turn to 5 or 6 only. Approve within a month rather than two year as before.

Hin[119] and Lim earlier place), there are second round for The Straits Settlement.

vii. Langkawi – from ducks and buffaloes on the road, become international and maritime air show - LIMA plus international even Le Tour De Langkawi (bicycle racing)

viii. TV3 and privatise, National Grid become TNB (efficient and creating revenue rather than liability before)

ix. Guthrie back to Malaysia, F1 calendar etc.

x. One more thing a lot of people forget and no outcry for the failure of Mahathir, yeah that's right it is *'Feri Malaysia'* (Malaysia Ferry – between East and West Malaysia). It's failed!

    1. Why the people forget? Because buying times for the vessel it about two million during economic down turn and after the project failed sell it out for twenty eight million. Where is this money? Is it in his personal account?

    2. The fail is failed. Suppose Lim Kit Siang blood bleed crying until today[120]. The peoples are unfair and wicked. The only thing his son (Lim Guan Eng) can be benefit of the bridge. Lucky that time done it's only about 800 million (just double of Sabirin's satellite). Otherwise if like now how many billion will be? Indeed, bridge over trouble water.

xi. It is pity that old man the people not recognize him except villages' poor men. But one thing I notice I never hear any word or phrase to credit himself much less shouting, barking, howling, bragging (like other Malays) unlimited repeating. It is not necessary for him and maybe he had no time to cater that entire stupid thing because I founded[121] he had a lot of things to do much more until now – no holiday.

xii. I am from technical back-ground, if one can review and try to understand the MSC alone with all planning and infrastructure[122], it is inconceivable. Indeed, on the globe on your table just find

---

[119] Chen Man Hin is ex Democratic Action Party (DAP) chairman.

[120] Last time (maybe celebrating both) Lim Kit Siang made police reports against Mahathir to drive Proton Saga cross Penang Bridge without road tax and insurance. There is nothing much issue that time for opposition.

[121] since my childhood / primary school in his medical clinic Alor Star

[122] I had one full detail (as 1997) like FAQ answer up to cyber-criminal and digital signature

California, there is Silicon Valley. Then next is Kuala Lumpur. Wall Street Journal hails as 'East Silicon Valley'. (I'm talking about 1997. Now?....)

xiii. Another think he said he will not allow his son[123] to be active in politics (?) and government during his tenancy in office, inversely others. If no son, son in law or daughter it's could. So he will fair and not be in favour[124] as much as like Lim Kit Siang 'Dynasty' or anybody else.

xiv. After he no more in tenancy, his son still cannot? What the hell of Malaysian purely never see the good of others?

5.3.2 - BY CERTAIN POINT OF VIEW;

a. We suppose to talk about a million and million only within 'calculated risk' because we are very small from any point of view. If anything happen next generation will be able to recover back because the fundamental is there. But the fact we are talking about billion now, just 'inflated bubbles' surrounding. We are talking about big 'shit' since the actual is like monkey's ass. It is the real tremendous disaster than ever.

b. Any stupid and dump person can smell rat. It is such a 'terror' if any leader plundering the nation in broad daylight. If he walks past the grave of Sphinx, this devil too have his eyes wide open, and if he walks past the mummy of Pharaoh, that mummy will stand up give axed salute - most notorious devil after his era.

c. Mahathir is look like to be 'son of Tun Razak Hussein' (Second PM). But some others just biological son.

d. It is awkward if any leader to let his wife ahead in any part of administration. She just housewife (not minister or who) should stay back in any situation because the rightful second, third, fourth man (of the country) will be responsible. The good example is Imxxxx R. Marxxx – on Friday Sept 20, 1974 she (alone?) arrived in Peking to clear way for diplomatic relation.

---

[123] In simulate in style of Saidina Umar? It is the Muslim 2nd Caliph.

[124] Except Anwar (too much emphasis and a rocket speed on PM nurturing project) – another failure project. Due to misled and loses on his (Anwar) original principle of precious Islamic faith. It is good to refer to his ex-Islamic special adviser (3 ½ year from 1994-1997), Ustaz Wan Zahidi Wan Teh, septuagenarian now, last a few years as 'mufti' in Kuala Lumpur. Or alternatively refer to News; MM 31st October, 1999 p7 – an interview, 'jangan glamorkan ulama'.

On Friday Sept 27, 1974 she met chairman Mao Tse-tung (Mastika, 1974, p. 63 & 68). Is it her job? Secondly; Friday to Friday, shopping? Some more alone! Who bear the cost? All of this will be questionable.

e. The Good and the Bad.

    i. The Good Guys: God will test you and torture you, but will not abandon you.

    ii. The Crooks n' No Good Ones: God will give you whatever you lust for, but at the end, will abandon you. Maybe like Marxxx and Imxxxx of Philxxxxxx or Pharaoh of Egypt. They want 3,000 pair of shoes they can; they want 20 million worth of ring they can, they want executive jet they can, but crossing the Red Sea they cannot.

f. If someone everyday everywhere shouting that his 'cork' as hard as cucumber but for the fact it is impotence, for what?

g. Is it the warrior, very dramatic kick to our own goal, with a big reward from 'unknown'?

h. Malay toward; 'everything does is illegal and prohibit.

    i. If a lorry capsizes, there a lot of Malays like vultures rush for carcass shameless and relentless. Double victimize for the lorry.

    ii. Dr Osman and vitamin. One practical Malay Muslim minded physician in Perlis, let me name him as Dr Osman had been ask why he not keep 'certain' vitamin. Under his prescription he asks to buy from pharmacist. He said he is panel doctor for some institutions. Unfortunately he comes to know the patients simply get the vitamin and sells off. No clarity.

i. Admonishing is cruel if you think so. But there also cruel to be good – worse like father canning[125] the son for not praying.

j. Dr Mahathir runs the nation; 55% corporate tax gradually down to maybe 35% now. But it tremendously creates much more revenue instead - 'lost but gain'. He 'grow' the money not like ordinary people does but his successors are the kings of harvester for lock stock and barrel. Putrajaya Symphony la……and a lot of people know. It is going to bankrupt.

---

[125] Canning and cruel - Prophet Muhammad asks to do so. At the end there is no father, no canning but the son continuously pray (mean he washes his face, hand & feet 5 time per day – good isn't it?) and this time to the grandchild. So what do you want to say about admonishing and cruel? Very subjective isn't it?
Is commando training cruel? You have choice to be trained in hotel air-condition room plus chicken chop or roasted chicken (not a snakes or monitor lizard) as dinner, sleeping bed and hot shower? For more discussion, see 7.5 – Canning and Cruel

k. Hospital and doctor mutually exist. But hospital is not for a doctor, for patients. Malaysian PM is neither not for his wife nor for his own sake?

l. Kolish, just 16 year old, son of Sis, one of wise religious man also bureaucrat, *'penghulu'*[126] for the biggest territory, *'Mukim Bebar'* in Pekan parliamentary area, was said to his friend in front of my son, "If you are so stupid, 'please keep some'".

   i. How do we feel if we are as Malaysia Prime Minister? Compare to the 16 year old boy; spend out all till everybody knows how stupid we are?

m. *'Skim Khidmat Siswazah'* (SKS) Mahathir; the concept?

   i. During Mahathir tenancy, it's about 1985 there was economic down turn. He adopts a scheme was named SKS, to help unemployed fresh graduate. The journalist asked him why just for graduate and not ordinary school certificate. He said 'these groups will have more damaging power[127] to the country'.

   ii. Suppose this will create us very far deep thinking and elaborations if we are.

n. Let see my clan! How the real statesman way of thinking – **'lateral thinking'** is an option, exactly like Tun Abd Razak for example on 'racial riot 1969'[128],

   i. To all Malay leaders!.... you shouldn't think just like small boy, direct thinking, spoon-up to poor man to show your courtesy. Your salary is not cheap to do that kind of task. If like that anybody can become prime minister or minister. World is very challenging now.

   ii. Just like 12 years old boy with only and the only have **'straight vertical logic'** playing rubber band, marble, worse no listen to the good idea and choose the only arse-licker, it mean a factory with no QC.

---

[126] *'Penghulu'* is a head for a group of villages to form *'mukim'*. They are bureaucrat.

[127] '..Damaging power'- it would be if they (graduates) had nothing to do like now because they are clever. If they are need to be a robber sure not just stealing chicken egg. It could be 'miracle task' to vanish a million dollars car within a few second in front of a thousand visitors in International motor show. If involve with cash, they will go multi million dollars with 'super un natural planning

[128] 'Racial riot 1969' - Tun Razak is not go to every Chinese with vertical logic, "you must good to Malay, so we can live peacefully" and to Malay reversely but he sees on his 'lateral thinking' – economic planning because this is the actual problem.

iii. What is 'straight vertical logic'? No money, give some money. No food, send rice, flour, sugar and salty fish. Low class income of citizen Malay leaders treat like a 'paralyse old man', spoon-up the porridge to show of courtesy. Then give underwear, taxi tyres.

5.3.2.1 - Quarrelsome of Mahathir

1. Some Malay leaders were said like this; "First, it was with Tunku Abdul Rahman (whom Dr M said) was wrong, Tun Hussein Onn...was wrong, Tun Musa Hitam...was wrong, Tun Abdullah Ahmad Badawi...was wrong.

   a. Indeed we must judge the content of the matter. Don't just blanket him as quarrelsome. We must ask, 'is there any substance in what he was bringing out?' Is he really mad or senile?[129] Any possibility may occur. Don't forget to classical children comic 'Hunter and his dog'. The hunter is stymied from dangerous snake since him too eager to his prey (top priority?). The dog is wrong? Then you kill the dog?

2. For me, that only local scale – too small. I also agree with Datuk Najib, all must be his 'head'[130]; Paul Keeting Australia was wrong (Mahathir is a hard-headed; but Malaysian proud of that - dauntless), Commonwealth was wrong (too much wasting time) M.Thatcher was wrong (unethically to raise our student fees in England & unethical and unfair embattlement tin future market), G. Soros was wrong (creature of Asian financial disaster), Camdessus (IMF prescription to 'slaughter' M'sia) was wrong, Israel was wrong (not allow him to enter Baitulmaqqdis), Singapore was wrong (for sending their military UAV cross-border to Johor), G.Bush was wrong (invaded Iraq)....... All subjects must be his 'head'. Indeed! Quarrelsome, world scale. He also wrong (to M.Thatcher) to 'bring back' Guthrie to Malaysia and his 'look east', he also wrong (to Camdessus) to turn down IMF prescription, and........ he also (done the biggest) wrong to waste Inland Revenue to help Malay (they only prone to outcast) because,

---

[129] I don't think he either mad or senile. Otherwise he easily can vanish. On contrary that why a lot of people worry to him. We should remember the isolation between very clever men and mad just as thin as onion skin. For example just see how a brilliant top judge talk and define. A lot of geniuses look like that (mad or senile) especially if he surrounded and interpreted by stupid community. Then who we are?

[130] He must be a man with principle – whatever and whoever wrong must be wrong. He doesn't care even if majority. That is why he always alone.

"......the Malays have apparently learnt nothing from the near loss of their country in the past -----Tun Dr. Mahathir Mohamad: The New Malay Dilemma - JANUARY 24, 2008 BY DINOBEANO. Worst thing they still blatantly never learn their loss of Singapura.

3. He 'quarrel' with **Tun Salleh Abas (Lord President)**

   a. So many assumptions especially against government and UMNO.

   b. Tun Salleh had not been biased against the Government. In numerous cases his judgement favoured the Government.

   c. None of those is true,

   d. He did complaint about the government. Two public speeches were delivered on 1st August 1987 and 12th January 1988[131]. The government not take action against him.

      i. "I must admit that Tun Salleh's complaints against me in his letter annoyed me. It is true that I had criticised the judges for interpreting the laws passed by Government not in accordance with **the intention or objective of the laws**. I did suggest that if the laws were interpreted differently from what the Government and the legislators intended, then we would **amend the laws**", Dr Mahathir.

      ii. "I also criticised judges for **making laws themselves** through their interpretations and subsequently **citing these as their authority**. I believed that the separation of powers meant the Legislators make laws and the judiciary apply them. Of course if the laws made by the legislators breach the provisions of the constitution, the supreme law of the land, then **judges can reject them**" continue Dr Mahathir.

   e. **But Tun Salleh's letter[132] to the King was dated 26th March 1988.**

   f. The truth is that the case against Tun Salleh was triggered by his letters to the Yang di Pertuan Agong which were considered by the Agong as being highly improper and insulting to him.

   g. In his first letter Tun Salleh had written to DYMM YDP Agong **complaining about the noise made during some repair work at the Agong's palace near Salleh's house.**

---

[131] For a full detail please refer to 'The Tun Salleh Saga' in Dr M blog chedet 6/6/2008.
[132] The letter was problematic one. It was too far from his earlier complaint to government.

h. This alone can be considered as very improper. A man as senior as he was could have asked to see the Agong and verbally informed him about the noise.

i. But to compound the act of les majesté he sent copies of his letter to the other rulers. This implied that he did not have faith in the Agong and wanted the other Rulers to apply pressure on him.

j. During one of my weekly meetings with the Agong, DYMM expressed his annoyance over the letters and simply requested that I dismiss Tun Salleh Abas from being the Lord President of the Malaysian Courts. **He writes in his own handwriting his request on the margin of Tun Salleh's first letter**, regarding the noise made by the work on the Agong's residence.

k. Another letter to DYMM YDP Agong complaining about the behaviour of the executive i.e. the Prime Minister. Copies of this letter were also sent to the other Rulers.

l. He went on to say in his letter "the accusations and comments have brought shame to all of us and left us mentally disturbed to the extent of being **unable to discharge our functions orderly and properly**."

m. Another point raised-up by himself.

n. In Section 125 of the Federal Constitution, under clause (3) the grounds for removing a judge, apart from misbehaviour include infirmity of body or mind or any other cause, properly to discharge the functions of his office."

o. **By his own admission** Tun Salleh was not able "to discharge his functions orderly and properly." He was therefore **unfit to continue to be a judge**.

p. Section 125, Clause 4 provides for "the Yang di Pertuan Agong to appoint a Tribunal …. and refer the representations to it, and may on the recommendation of the tribunal remove the judge from office."

q. I was very concerned over the forcible removal of Tun Salleh. And so I tried to get Tun Salleh to resign on his own so as to avoid a scandal. He agreed at first but he withdrew the following day.

r. Upon the Agong agreeing, the Government selected six judges and former judges for His Majesty to consider. The members included foreign judges in the person of the Honourable the Justice K.A.P. Ranasinghe, Chief Justice Democratic Socialist Republic of Sri Lanka and the Honourable Mr Justice T.S. Sinnathuray, Senior Judge of the Supreme Court of Singapore.

s. The Chairman was the Chief Judge (Malaya), Tan Sri Dato Abdul Hamid bin Hj Omar. The other members were Dato Sri Lee Hun Hoe, Chief Justice (Borneo), Tan Sri Abdul Aziz bin Zain, Retired Judge and Tan Sri Mohd Zahir bin Ismail, Retired Judge.

t. The inclusion of foreign judges was to make sure the Tribunal would not be biased.

u. I then went about getting the Tribunal approved and set up. Naturally I had to consult the Attorney-General and others who were familiar with judges. **Once the Tribunal was set up my involvement ended**.

v. Pity the old man Mahathir:-

    i. "I write this to record things as they happened. I do not expect my detractors to stop saying that I destroyed the judiciary. They are my prosecutors and they are also my judges. To them I will always be the Idi Amin of Malaysia as claimed in Tun Salleh's book "May Day for Justice". Sadly many who so readily condemn me were judges"[133]

w. In this case (Tun Salleh Abas, Lord President), it look like Mahathir was 'victimise' by public opinion. If we go through to the book of Tun Salleh himself **'TUN SALLEH ABAS – KEBEBASAN KEHAKIMAN** – Singa di bawah takhta dijerat (satu kezaliman)' in 1989 we can see the 'truth'.

    i. On page 337, second paragraph he (Tun Salleh) said himself that he had proof the idea of his dismissal is from the King (Yang di-Pertuan Agong). His letter to the King makes him angry.

    ii. It was strongly seconded by pages 324 – 328 – 'Dismissal due to angry?' On page 327 last paragraph line 10, he said his explanation was unacceptable by the King[134] and he was asking to resign. On page 328 he had sufficient time to throw his tantrum to the King, "I won't resign. If dismissed, my livelihood is rest in the hand of Allah. If no choice I had no shame to return to plant potatoes in my village"

4. He 'tries to quarrel' with Barack Obama; Open letter to Obama.

a. The only thing was Obama is clever. Indeed, naturally!

---

[133] Please take note there a lot of explanation if you need in 'Tun Salleh Saga' in chedet's blog.

[134] In Johor, June 27, 1988

    b. He wrote an open letter[135] somewhere around Jan 2009 or December 2008 about 9 issues to do or stop that and this. Among that, do signing Kyoto Protocol and others treaties, do respect to United Nations. Stop casino that US regard as financial institution, among that the banks should stop issuing loan of billion dollars from non-existence money.

    c. He no more prime minister for whom he do that? Why not he sleeps or relaxes and why he likes to 'work'? What principle he had? We need to understand him first before try to test him.

    d. Surely 'Be warrior until die' isn't it?

5.3.2.2 - Why Dr Mahathir could stay in the office for 22 years?

1. Why and how he resign? Is he incompetent, the peoples no more support him, the peoples topple him down or too many peoples lust for the post with prosperous[136] under his reign from poor nation depends on rubber and tin to new emerge industrial country?

2. Why this was no answer? "UMNO can make a statement about the money I gave to Dato Abdullah when I stepped down. Better still Dato Abdullah can explain how much of the 1.4 billion Ringgit in cash, shares and property that my staff and one of his Ministers handed over to him is still with him". Definitely he wants to please and make his successor's life easy isn't it? Unfortunately he nurtures ingrate formidable adversary Beelzebub or Prince of Darkness. Back stabbed! Exactly like successful businessman hand-over to ungrateful son (and don't know how to run business) then enjoy (with cash – for symphony, fiesta as priority and so on) and plunder up the properties/assets and facing up to bankrupt.

3. How he (Dr M) manages and holding 'cash', why he or his wife or his sons or step-son (if any) not plunder that 1.4 billion?

4. Why not he handed over with empty coffer to Abdullah and let Abdullah 'search for the money'? It is not too late he has enough time to plunder that particular amount as he had confirms one year before his resignation. Is he stupid? Let we guess.

---

[135] Malay news, Utusan Malaysia Jan 2, 2009; it also uploaded in his blog *www.chedet.co.cc.*

[136] It was proved by non-stop foreigner come (plus illegal way) to join in the prosperous of the country and he could manage to hand-over 1.4 billion cash to his successor Abdullah Badawi.

5. Why Rafidah, Hishamuddin and other UMNO leaders 'hold' him not to resign at the moment. Instead ask him to stay, negotiated then one more year? From my opinion I can see his sincerity and his disenchanted with his failing to 'change' the Malay after so long time. Many attempts were failed. He no more can hide (from non-Malay) and cannot continue on heavy bias supporting to Malay since the Malay never show sign of changing. Sure he feels shame and no ability to apply 'full brake' to Chinese in order to wait for Malay which no move at all except amusement, fiesta, over-acting, over-proud, corruption[137], wrong-doing and mostly **'over-price'**. Since kindergarten and standard six (12 years old primary school) have great grand 'convocation'. Pity Malay, **celebrating and ceremony clan**.

All discussion here is strictly for the country and the Malay who are prone to become 100% full liability which against their religious. Don't worry **this is not to credit to Dr Mahathir** but it was implied as what he has done before. We cannot be constant self-denial to the histories.

5.3.2.2.1 My point of view;

He must be a man with principle – whatever and whoever wrong must be wrong. He doesn't care even if majority. That is why he always alone. While others are 'fluctuating' he is still resolute with the truth and principle. To clear view for Malay Muslim, you can see your Prophet Muhammad. He alone (he don't care) to upright his principle and finally like we all know. I see another principle is 'be warrior until die' especially when you are facing 'disaster'. Even you are so old how can you ignore / sleep if you are feel like cross-country or rally in your most comfortable coach.

On the issue of 'Dr M meets Anwar after 18 years';

He is there to give credence and support over Anwar's deed against National Security Council (NSC). He is not there to ask for forgiveness over his wrongdoings towards Anwar in 1996.

Indeed! True. He is the great man with the great principle - lesson to young generation. **The truth is truth**. He (Dr M) doesn't care either enemy or not. Then he go out to that particular issue ONLY and keep sided other issue(s) if against to main agenda. It is much less to his earlier issues (same stage with opposition) to

---

[137] The Malay will get world recognition THE FIRST TOP in CORRUPTION.

topple PM (ONLY). We must learn from his principle not to mix-up (sometime personal matter) or on denial mode just because 'the truth' is from your nemesis like oppositions did. It is now transmissible to UMNO – constantly denial (like Nazri Aziz) though vitally blatantly sublimely facts. Be gentleman and civilize like European. Be cooperating even like loose scrum (in rugby) for the nation. Fight by the issue not by the group. See the wolf, they always 'quarrel' but when a tiger try attacking them they will surround and counter attack and the tiger MUST run away. Then continue to quarrel don't mix-up the tiger issue.

It is one good thing to consider about 'the truth is truth'; **If Satan said 'if you follow me against the God you will land up to the hell'** you must concede it even he is your enemy.

Another point I like to view is GOOGLE.

How they survive?

I guess by;

1) Giving free service to the whole world especially poor one.
2) Then they become well known and trusted for every inches of the world.
3) Any business (maybe advertisement) they want to venture after that become easy peasy. Every party like to join in.

The only brilliant brain can see universe far of distance and not like most Malay leaders just short sighted.

When they (Malay leaders except Mahathir) in financial difficulties they will screw-up poor one to suck dry the blood. They cannot go far, on the contrary their Prophet Muhammad very love to poor peoples and taught they (poor peoples) are your wealthy. They can't see the implied.

Google and Communist of China may learn, analyse and maybe inadvertently come to this Islamic taught and success.

5.3.3 - ANY LEADERS;

i. We should avoid full time embattlement with 'rakyat'. Dimwit would say we are stupid like theirs. Then they said they also can be PM and like to 'challenge' you on their stupid preaching.
ii. Sometime if we misappropriate 'sentence' to our 'enemy' and deny their right and livelihood, it could make worse instead; because we land them to 'nothing to do'. Consequences too much time to attack and disturb

us back because no work and they are not stupid like us. Everyday politicking.

    i.   Look how Mahathir handle Lee Kim Sai. His garrulous[138] make Sultan of Selangor recall back his 'dato'ship'. That time he was MCA[139] youth. Then Mahathir appoint him as minister (maybe Health) as can see from daily newspaper he not even enough time to comb his hair. The effect, MCA was 'diverted' from the never ending issue like the Malay's favourite does – Like now, 24/7/365 politicking.

    ii.   Still with Mahathir, he took back 'B team' Rais Yatim, Abdullah Badawi (Ingrate old folk finally torn flesh and become **'the father of the Malay ruination'** – the biggest mistake of Mahathir), and others with his renown phrase; **'Winner is not win all and loser is not lose all' – grandeur the exalted leader.** Softness of practical Muslim. Somehow rather it was dissented by Daim (Finance Minister) as he doesn't believe the gang then become true – ingrated!

  iii. He was sincerely to develop the nation not for his own sake. Otherwise, Proton 'so obviously open' will be 'Mahathir and Sons' isn't it? Right now he totally 'loose' Proton. In contrary normally for example like Rossington[140]. How many contractors were kill and how big? How about 'Kraftangan'? How many companies wind up? This kind of small thing should be protected their right and taken care by authority and not to plunders up? Just livelihood.

5.3.4 - DROP-OUT

1)   Bill Gate dropped out (?) of Harvard University, then become top billionaire

2)   In 1984, Michael Dell dropped out of college and started a computer company. He was 19. Then Dell Computer one of the world's largest technology company, with $33 billion in annual sales and its founder is one of the world richest men. Fortune.com has named Dell the wealthiest American under 40 with asset worth of $16.5 billion (Newsweek October 21, 2002)

---

[138] He try to resolute to deny Malay as indigenous (also immigrant)

[139] MCA = Malayan Chinese Association is one of a component party of Barisan Nasional (BN) a government

[140] Rossington – the company in deal with bore water prospecting for aborigine offspring in Pekan, Pahang

3) I also drop out of Universiti Kebangsaan Malaysia (UKM) so I also same as Bill Gate and Michael Dell? Ha ha ha…maybe! But actually I purely drop flat and ash less totally burned up.
   a. Then I am the most outstanding among three, isn't it?
   b. Yes! It is the most outstanding debt.
   c. Never mind whatever the word is, the fact is the fact.
   d. The earlier discussion on SKS (above) is slightly related. I am not as same as typical kampong man (the man who never goes higher studies at all). I will have difference question and responsibility from the God to answer depend on my capacity even I am not degree holder.
   e. I also can write even not as well as degree holders but I still difference with that typical kampong man.
   f. It shows Mahathir and SKS is truly right.

5.4 - Life Is Going On To Be Outcast

All bad elements will continue to penetrate into the Malay cultures because they cannot resists their psychological needs. Many want to get rich quick. Endless corruption, kick back, commission makes Malays lazy. All classes of people including the royal elites are not free from these bad elements. It's already been a culture.

The Chinese takes full advantage of these weaknesses. They who came in with single pant and a hat to plant vegetable, or pulling trishaw and/or disposing human waste so to speak, had already made their fortune whereas the Malays still hovering themselves with some small time fishing, carpentering, or petty trading.

Chinese were regarded as non-citizen in their parents' time. (Only those born after independence got citizenship rights) they got their citizenship by grace of the local district officer.

As years went by, we saw them taking their hats off (hat-labourer symbol). They switched profession to petty businessman and later started acquiring small plots of land to build some sort of small workshops. In the later years in a blink of seconds their workshops turn to ware houses busy as ever. Many previously were from the emergency camps (camps build by the British during emergency) now flocked in towns and cities. Majority of the Malays were still wearing the cultural gear, the Batik Sarongs, staying in villages till this day. Only in recent years Malays took off their Batik Sarongs and clad in long pants and jeans.

Malays depend very much on Malay supremacy. Malays are still weak to face odds challengers unlike others. China, African, Philippines or even Indonesia they citizen could endure internal or external pressures. Malay need be treated like growing babies for survival. Thereby UMNO must be valid in order to keep Malay as dignified subjects. Malay supremacy must be alive otherwise they will be outcast citizen. Therefore unity is a secret thing. In this context Islamic faith play vital role.

That all for times being.

Just relax and let have the following 'High Tea'.

Chapter 2

HIGH TEA

Just be relaxed and let have this 'High Tea'.

PART 6.0 - HIGH TEA

6.1 - Lesson For Education Ministry

```
J046 - PERMISSION PENDING
------------------------
The Star 19/9/2014
Dorairai: Lesson for the Education Ministry – The UPSR
(std 6 examination) leak fiasco, too much emphasis on
scoring 'A'
```

141

I had no comment. It is compacted and very clear as he himself has a daughter with no A's

---

141 News, The Star, 19 Sept 2014, Education Ministry

6.2 - TNB Substation, Malacca

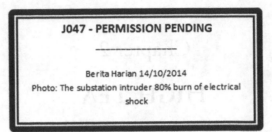

J047 - PERMISSION PENDING

Berita Harian 14/10/2014
Photo: The substation intruder 80% burn of electrical
shock

142

- No Brain
- 80% burned
- 1 hour black-out. Maybe some chaotic in town and on the road.
- Loss of RM 200k for Grid (TNB) and maybe some from small industries and so on. If he could steal something, how much he will get on sacrifices of a few hundred thousand?

By doing this it's should be outcast of the planet? For slightly better mean put in showcase and feed until die. Collect some cash (of ticket for feeding) from visitors definitely from Singapore, Taiwan, Hong Kong, mainly China. So they could admire the success of their ancient journey to take over Tanah Melayu (the Malay land) which is 'willingness' hand over peacefully to them.

For slightly smaller scale is like this;

VERTEX
Nano Hydrogen Water

How much an effort to do this, how much they get, & what the damage?

143

---

142   News, BH 14 Oct 2014, Substation's (Grid) intruder
143   ZP's, 2015, Nenasi Pekan

6.3 - 'Menberuk'[144] (Scrap Iron Mentality)

This acronym was suddenly flash due to the pressure in my mind about so many extremely stupid case of my clan.

Extremely stupid - I created two obvious examples here to easy understand.

Firstly; two boys (definitely Malay) steal one roll very high precision multicore cable (it worth about three thousand dollars) from pick-up van when the driver stops for a while to toilet. An agile leap of action less than half an hour the cable totally burn down to expose the metal. Let say within two hours the boys get caught and founded it was sold for twenty dollars scrap iron/metal.

Secondly; this is more obvious example;
A boy steal a Rolex watch it worth about fifty thousand dollars.
Then he smashes it to look as scrap iron and sell off for one dollar.

This is how 'Menberuk' is.
They only can see the metal (without anything else) and how to turn to scrap. It is worse than mouse in sewage-farm. That is Malay current activities and it is impairment to be majority in society. Whatever 'pariah'[145] criminalities are theirs.

How to say so?
Donation money box[146] in their mosque they can temper inconceivable, damage! If they could it is very small amount and not correspond to[147].

Anything can be connected to their 'menberuk' in that mosque[148] they will plunder up together at the same time. They cannot see far, don't care the consequences.

They never learn that to become a bandit still need 'rule'[149]. In the war there also law and rule to be adhere.

---

[144] 'Menberuk = Mentaliti Besi Buruk'
[145] 'Pariah' – low class in society
[146] Money box – actually a safe box with all dial code and all safety features.
[147] Correspond to the above case TNB Substation.
[148] Their own mosque – consider like they fuck their own mother. Unlimited!
[149] Bandit - This you can see in the 'notorious robber' in last part of 1.5 - Malay Nationalism – Unity and Sovereignty.

This is the real meaning of *'Menberuk'*.

Sorry to everybody of my inadvertently invention of the word[150] which is reflect to the current situation which is bound to 'outcast' of Malay in reality.

6.3.1 - WATERWHEEL OF WINDMILL 'PASIR GUDANG'.

Current owner is *Majlis Perbandaran Pasir Gudang* [151](*MPPG*)

The original plan for this project was 'Educational Windmills'.

It was 2 set consisting of Rotors to drive the components for the big one (6.0m diameter) is waterwheel and generator (dynamo) and the small one (4.4m diameter) is screw pump.

I join the contractor in 1999 to handle installation and test run. The design was done and fabrication (in China) is in progress.

I had founded the design was not 'properly taken care' to some technical aspect. I only had opportunity to check (Pre Delivery Inspection) in China in August 2000.

It was affected more than 30 'major' changes I made[152]; some are not including in the system. All of the changes are my own design and I furnish the free drawing instead.

That time I was be 'all in one', no official time and 'round the clock';

I'm consultant, I'm engineer, I'm technician, I'm foreman, I'm designer, I'm draftsman, I'm office boy, I'm clerk, I'm supervisor, I'm QC, I'm negotiator to hardware and machine shop, I'm welder, I'm lorry driver, I'm porter, I'm wash man, I'm cleaning man & I'm also bouncer to protect the work.

---

[150] Invention of the word – the existence of any vocabulary is regarding to something surrounding for instance *'durian'* (Malaysia local fruit), it is not exist in Europe but in Malaysia.

[151] MPPG is one of the biggest municipal town council in Malaysia, situated in Johor.

[152] I cannot go to normal procedure because a lot of wasting time concern. Too much time just 'sleeping' or hibernate end up nothing happen. Another factor is very costly for this kind of small matter and for sure any consultant (normally big firm for this kind of cases) not interested. They cannot frequently assign an engineer, technician and so on to look for too small job like this, what will the cost like?

Finally most of the client staffs put everything rely on me because this is out of their scope. Every time to speak they will say 'your windmill' and they call me 'Zul windmill'. That is how so were to speak.

Barely after 3 years of my resignation from the contractor, have the windmill matters still wanted to follow me even I want to furnish a copy of certain related drawing for free. They ask me "how you make business, if the drawing you want to give to other people?"

That mean I got no choice they only trust me and they put this under 'specialist job' and direct negotiation deal – no tender out.

In 2008 one set of the blade bracket was broke and the blade was fallen down. I went to inspect and I make a full report with full detail of photographs (I have a lot of photos). Any officer need not necessary to climb up to inspect as a full detail plus zoom and arrow pointed to the defect shown in the appropriate photos.

Major repair was carried out.

Mainly rotor blade and frame of stainless steel I had changed. The blade I change to fibre glass in order to lighten the load on horizontal shaft and bearing (due to oblong effect on bearing housing – a lot of photograph I kept). At the same time alteration I made from twin waterwheel to single[154], in order to lighten overall load to the rotor.

---

[153] ZP's, 2008, Pasir Gudang

[154] Then we have extra one wheel and I plan to make sculpture. For education purpose, that can be motorized and equip with all related parameter equipment such volumetric/flow meter; torque, power and efficiency measurement. Then we can 'feel' comparison to it 'sibling' driven by wind energy. I could design but now gone by blatant 'menberuk' officer.

15/01/2008 155, 02/02 156

After that major repair, as the earlier as before I resign from the contractor, I was frequently emphasis verbally and more on writing for them to make routine maintenance. I already furnish them the schedule for maintenance and always remind, "You cannot always depend on me, old man, because if I am dying, how?"

They bounced back partially serious and joke, "If you die, I will scrap it out".

So I just shook the head. Nothing can say.

A lot of people consider that windmill as my mutual exist and as my baby.

Some sort like my baby, I still continue to remind them (in writing) with more emphasis and analogy, "If you not bother about to change engine oil, you would land up to change the engine". Just to changes one 'front bearing' you need to crane down and you need to park on 'base kit' as what I design. Its better take care of lubrication. Cheaper!

Within my expectation, about 2010 the problem is rise again but a bit lighter due to a lot of modification I had done.

This time I had to make 'base-kit[157]' again as the earlier one was sold as *'besi buruk'* (scrap iron) by officer in charge. It is after I traced out, on surefooted a Malay officer and tail me splash out the phrase *'menberuk'*

---

155   ZP's,2008,Pasir Gudang

156   Ibid

157   The kit I was design and make (with remarkable colour - orange) in order to receive top part of windmill during maintenance. It is considered as parking place after crane down and before to crane up.

Let see the photo. The orange base is base kit. It is purely my budget (no claim) worth about seven thousand inclusive design (if paid for). The only thing I design on my own and supervise fabrication out

After the shut-down job finished as the before I need to keep this base-kit[159] for next shut-down if any.

For me, it doesn't matter who will be assign especially if I die or not be able to do anymore. The important is the kit must be with client[161] (MPPG) as this will affect a lot of unnecessary job cannot buy from hardware shop.

---

[158]   ZP's,2010, P.Gudang

[159]   The kit was stored in engineering section beyond *'menberuk'* officer's interference with MPPG technician on 8 June, 2010)

[160]   ZP's,2010,P.Gudang

[161]   Previous set I stored in Klang is about 400 km away bound to KL. It is impractical too far keeping such that.

I purposely coloured in orange to avoid any mistake and it remarkable to hinder *'menberuk'* officer to pretend 'don't know'. Conspicuously I dare to put wire metal tag 'Don't sell or throw – Windmill property' and also I wrote on portal frame and tie up together.

Collectively.......promiscuous;

- Rigid like this can be mistaken sell off? – yes *'menberuk'* is

- Stainless steel is expensive – *'menberuk'*. Sold out! Distinctly!

Whose one doesn't care like the rat in sewage-farm or in a kitchen? Promiscuously!

162   ZP's,2010,P.Gudang
163   ZP's,2010,P.Gudang

- it is also thick stainless steel – *'menberuk'*. Must be sold out! Even the mother can sell cheap. Any offer?

- That big, custom made 2.4mØ, full calculation and experiment done in China, came to Malaysia as twin. After my modification to reduce load on rotor, the twin was detached to be single wheel left over another wheel and stationed in MPPG's store.

It is very admiring to *'menberuk'* officer 'Lustfulness' vigorously, agile, the blood pressure increasingly and cannot stand anymore.

What's the hell?

---

164   ZP's,2008, P.Gudang
165   ZP's,2008, P.Gudang
166   ZP's,2008,P.Gudang

Yeah.........once I received a call[167] (28/12/2009) from one of MPPG officer, related to windmill En Anuar Abd Ghani. I was currently in Kedah that time.

"Your water wheel the people want to sell, already up on the lorry"

"Hah?" I asked.

"Don't worry, lucky we see. I ask them to take it down. It is belonging to windmill".

I am so worried because the villain is inside and 'powerful enough'.

The only thing it was lucky he hasn't enough power to sell municipal building or MPPG itself or to sell Johor at once. Otherwise he will vomit blood by the Sultan. One to remember this windmill was very concern by the late Sultan of Johor, DYMM Sultan Iskandar.

Not long just after that within one or two weeks it was sold out instead. How much it worth?

It is about two hundred thousand engineering value.

This is highly technical value[168] inside with long process R&D and some more shipped from abroad. This is national scale talk. How many such windmills we had compare to how many Proton car we have in Malaysia. Parts replacement is not like ordinary cars replacement. Be patriotic laaa…please!

this broken bracket[170] had to make / custom made. It is not cheap anyway.

---

167 Double calls– Dec 28, 2009;
   16:52:44hrs, duration 07:54min; suddenly cut-off, then
   17:01:16hrs, duration 02:50min. {Do you need the phone numbers to check?}

168 Technical value – smooth and 'perfect' balance – no vibration. They tested with vibration in the lab. So to the rotor, they make testing in wind tunnel and refine it, otherwise the whole building of that kites museum will feel vibration and nuisance. To think; how about the balancing of your car's tires? How small the palette is? To think some more; from end to end of big aircraft wing (like Boeing or Airbus) the tolerance is less than one mm (about 0.3mm).

169 ZP's,2007, P.Gudang

170 Bracket for holding the blade – It is about six hundred dollar to fabricate. You need plasma cutting machine beside the plate itself, needed to roll, stainless steel welding

Hey 'menberuk' officer, your success on windmill is emboldening you. I would like to remind you don't keep on going your ways of thinking then you will predispose to sell our submarines as a scrap iron because it is too early and to acquire that it maybe how many costly surreptitious meeting then Malaysian suffer rather than relief of maybe colossal amount dirty money involvement.

It could be claim to death if anything wrong. Your body will turn to micron powder, not even ash. So braggart you are?

Back to waterwheel, do we think this 'menberuk' officer will get kick back of hundred thousand? or hundred fifty thousand? Maybe it is about 150 dollars instead.

As what we would think from this 'menberuk' officer;........

"What the hell of this old Rolex watch. My father uses it for more than fifteen years". In his opinion a watch is only thirty five dollars.

Then he get ten dollar from scrap iron merchant. The only thing he not smashes it to look like scrap iron otherwise twenty cents only. Then his friend is the world cleverest scrap iron merchant indeed. Or on other version it is just stupidity of 'scrapped' Malay before his outcast.

That is what the value added to do to that such amount of metal (for Rolex watches). 'Brain watches' not 'metal watches'.

Anyway This 'Menberuk' officer should steals off twenty million worth of ring and sells it to his intimate friend (that particular scrap iron merchant) for twenty dollars.

20 million to 20 ringgit (dollar).

Those were how to speak 2020.

Then oust for outcast with that 20 ringgit.

It is to summarise this officer real super wicked. This is not a mistake at all. First try he was failed then he try for second time and success.

6.4 - The Cows And Cross Country. Half Boiled.

This is the Pekan parliamentary area. One can see where the cows? They are everywhere in the village, housing area, under the shed, bus stop, cross the road and so on

---

machine beside an expert and a hell lot of grinding works. Each blade you need two pieces but difference shape and time 12 pieces of blades. So you can buy a good secondhand car with that fourteen thousand. So what the hell you sell **'that Rolex'**.

171,

172,

173.

---

171   ZP's, Oct 2010, Nenasi Pekan
172   ZP's, Nov 2010, Nenasi Pekan
173   ZP's, Jan 2013, Nenasi Pekan

It faeces everywhere.

174, 175

What they have? It don't care what or whose. The whole planet is theirs.

176

The lady 'crying'. How many years she fence and take care, suddenly a group of cows break through and eat all these. Unfortunately she was not a home.

Firstly, the question is what kind of Muslim they are. Half boiled / half cooked fuckwit Muslim of Malay. their Prophet Muhamad with very strong emphasis in last 'khutbah'(preach) 'don't hurt peoples'

2nd – How much the growth of cow after destroys that much of plant. It's one kilogram?

3rd – Is Muslim Malay peoples are no brain like that cows? They want the whole world to be carpet for them as they no slipper?

174 ZP's, Aug 2010, Nenasi Pekan
175 ZP's, Dec 2015, Nenasi Pekan
176 ZP's, 2015,Nenasi Pekan

How much 'crying' is this?

You just imagine how suffer of this traveller together with wife and children, more than hundred kilometre to go. Towing alone (now on board) is about RM500 simply burned case. Most of these cases (towing) is not eligible to the claim. Stranded time and so many problems. Coming will another one or two or three months the car to be in workshop. If hospitalise and some more with physical disability or die?

It is inconceivable the ratio between damage and benefit if you are normal human being.

This is more severe case. We no need to discuss as 4 cows in one go and die. Real suffering …

The authority never thinks to overall citizen.

Just the matter of thinking, clarity, obeys God, Obey their own Prophet.
As said before they are just half boiled practice of their own believe, Islam …

---

177   ZP's, Sept 2015, Nenasi Pekan
178   ZP's, Apr 2013, Nenasi Pekan

6.5 - Self-Indulge R&D Only Less Than 2%

J054 - PERMISSION PENDING	J055 - PERMISSION PENDING
———————	———————
Berita Harian 14/10/2014 Headline – R&D	Berita Harian 14/10/2014 R&D – Grant for universities spending chart

, 179

There only less than 2% R&D's of 15 universities be commercialise within 5 to 10 years after certain billion finishes as grant.

R&D's is not easy but I like so much within my scale. Its challenge and we will be inconceivable 'award' on completion.

180

6.5.1 - TILE CUTTING MACHINE

This machine is my own design and build. That kind of features (cutter moves instead of tile moves) was request by client and not available in market. After the success they order for second unit.

R&D for what the people want sure can market easily. Alternatively you must create marketing strategy if the thing is worthwhile.

For technical person they can see my problem, the necessary of big pulley to drive smaller one in order to increase of speed (to suit the cutting disc operational

---

179 Both - News BH, 14 Oct, 2014, R&D
180 ZP's,1999,Klang

speed) definitely will be lack of power – selection of motor problem because the client insist for single phase. It was one unit of motor burn down on this trial.

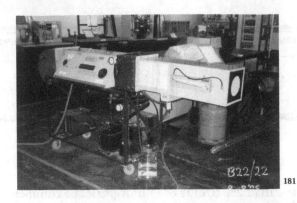

This one B22/22 is Didactic, air conditioner trainer for one of polytechnic POLIMAS in Jitra at Kedah.

The machine, England originate was 15 years abundance as some of the part is obsolete. I took the manual and study and compare for equivalence. After long survey in market, finally I got one (refrigerant / hermetic compressor) nearest and almost within their range for student purposes. I need full scale of experiment[7] on this new compressor in order to cover the range, to plot new test curve, lab sheet and videos for the student. It was done, 2 units completed.

If they have budget I can digitise all thermometers and flow meters. So real time or recorded data is obtainable in soft copy. It's transferable throughout the world yet auto report feature can be design for.

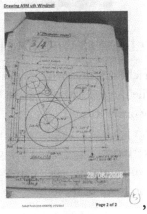

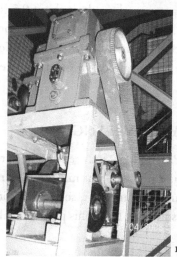

182, 183

6.5.2 - ASM (ALTERNATOR SPEED MECHANISM)

This is what I call ASM and it is my Design & Build. That time I still need to draft in a graph paper.

A lot of time consume in designing only late 2008 I be able to use computer after 2 days x 9 hours learning time. I'm very lucky to get one to one teaching style by just clever teenager boy who knows to cover up all important aspects and sample in one go. Finally he said, whatever I teach you within two continuous days, we had to learn in two semesters (about one year).

It took a lot of precaution as the space very limited (even no room for tensioner and must be void) and existing coordinates on the bridge of existing dynamo have to follow. Whatever hardware needed has to buy first due to critical dimension.

---

182 All 4 - ZP's, Apr 2008, Pasir Gudang Johor
183 ZP's, June 2008, Pasir Gudang Johor

This is my own idea to create this one. It was because the original system is very big (on higher side) and most of the time is fail due to small wind blow.

If just for education it better small scale and could run most of the time. I think to change for a motorcar alternator (dynamo). It is very cheap, just common knowledge (auto mechanics only) and accessible from anywhere. The second-hand serviced one it about RM100 not RM50, 000 or RM60, 000. The car battery is only about RM 200 and not like original battery it worth about RM45, 000. The problem is the car alternator working speed should be around 1,500 RPM but windmill nominal output just about 200 RPM. That is the purpose of ASM to increase speed about 10 times. Finally I get a good result, it about 9.5 times.

That kind of small thing (R&D's) still carry a lot of works and cost. It is very heavy load to me as every cent must come from my own pocket. Moreover anything like petrol even groceries must be taken care. How good if comes from a grant as researcher (universities) does.

6.5.3 - UMP (UNIVERSITI MALAYSIA PAHANG)

My proposals which I was sent to UMP last 3 years maybe straight to rubbish dump. It really full hard works in poverty as daily need was miss out like nobody business no sponsor and nothing. That maybe can hope something, it never happen. It was colourful of hard copy and soft copy (CD plus professional glossy label) supplied for free.

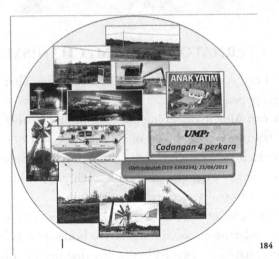

It was:

---

184   ZP's, Sept 2013, Proposal (to UMP) CD label.

6.5.3.1 - 'Industri Padi' (Paddy industries)

- This is long story[185]. Test me! It was here just the sketch of how look like the industrial lot is. This is for everybody no restriction, no patent or some sort like that. Just universal for human being which are belong to the God. If anything benefit it just for us and plus day after for a Muslim faith.

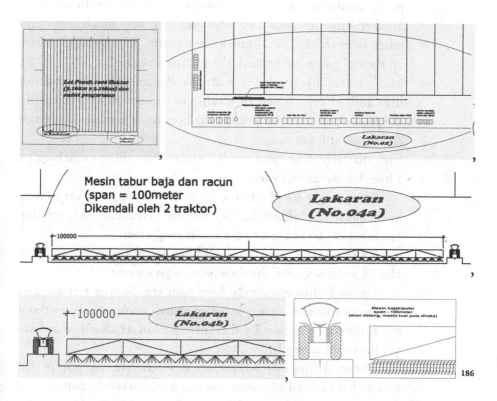

---

[185] I had very detail tasks on paddy planting write-up (as given to UMP) from the person who is exponentially success since he start in Kedah and Perlis last a few years. He also design and fabricate his own machinery in home yard. His earlier trade was in heavy machinery and shipping maintenance in Johor especially. I call him 'professor' because he never misses out his 'research'. He calculates everything (that what I got from his write-up) and he measure in quantitative value as well as qualitative on his plant growth and machinery usage, wear and tear, cost rate per area and so on. He dares to talk as he 'hand-on' up to gangsters' and foreign workers affair. This is very exclusive thing never in the book.

[186] All 5 - ZP's, Aug 2013, Own Design & Drawing – Paddy Industry. It is an idea during five years (2004 - 2009) in Kedah in gathering with that 'professor'.

- One can compare this to 1000 Ha (?) existing (20 over years) prawn farm (plus factory) in Datuk Seri Najib (PM) parliamentary area Pekan. It is Agrobest Sdn Bhd (formerly was Song Cheng). You can surf aerial view through Google and can see how the lot of one hectare each of arrangement.
  o I make comparison in my proposal and forecast the calculation of paddy production in term of million dollar and return (as 2009 'market' of paddy price and subsidise). It is very much easier and much more efficiency and much more return. The assumption base on the real ground of numerical and experience had.
  o Much better this project is gradually change from now and not drastically change. Albeit of waiting to the system to accomplish, the production as earlier (even better because of manageable lot size and shape) still can run.

Even that technology need to fail it's no matter, still can wait because a huge benefit already there.

The straight lot of 3km x 100m x 29 rows will 'very much much much more' effective, efficiently due to tractors and harvesting machines can go straight under one management.

So with irrigation control will be easier. One can put aside my idea of 'aerial operated' for time being even for ever.

I'm sure after everybody have seen the lot, the farmers and spectators will talk about 'aerial operated' automatically without any influence of outside. By that time one can see clearly what I am talking about currently.

The good thing I already prepare to 'receive' the emerging of that idea with the related infrastructure was done – it is dyke cum as road for prime mover to move and for any other possibilities. That we can consider as 'well plan' – to be prepare for any forth coming possible idea to come through.

'Aerial operated system' will help on reducing the labour case and danger[187] case (poison) and also reliability of evenness of spray fertilizer and poison

---

[187] Poison – a lot of cases. It takes long time like cancer to affect lung and such problem. The people scared and mostly uneducated poor man will do this dangerous job.

We can design to put two units of air-condition booths to spray poison or fertilizer. It travel 50 meter each on girder from left to right and back.

Then paddy planters will works on safety boots, heavy machineries, proper workshop, store, R&D and control room and maybe control tower. The leg not even wet. This will attract more educated people to jump in. Their brain can use not only bull power. Note: See what IBM[188] did on agriculture in Brazil. So what the computer and ICT do now? Open our mind and look forward. A little deviation of Vision 2020 to agriculture still never mind if we can go on technologies.

6.5.3.2 - Solar Park (not solar farm).

Solar Park is where the solar kits are on individual roof. Normal one is solar farm. It's not attractive, very private and exclusive. Test me!

6.5.3.3 - Windmill.

- Basic and bulky windmill is better for beginning. Later then be delicate or advance.
- All level can see. From small boy until professor.
  - o Good exposure. Children will have an idea or experience since then.
  - o For education purposes it better for anybody have to see Pilatus PC7 (pilot aircraft training) for example rather than straight to Airbus 380. You only can see the wealthy not the engine and so on.
  - o I can create (infrastructures) the challenge for the researcher. Test me! The analogy is like this if I can make racing car but I cannot race.
- Simply can 'touch' and feel it rather than complicated one.

6.5.3.4 - Geophysics

It is the best state for the subject, Pahang. Recently a landslide was in the UMP state, in Cameron Highland. Genting Highland and a few that such kinds of places were in Pahang. The highest mountain also is in Pahang.

There a lot of potential places to be monitor.

---

188   IBM and Brazil - please see 6.5.5.1 - Precision Agriculture and this video will help to show https://youtu.be/qVn9FOnRSHg

My idea is to lowering down the task to the proper hands. Like now doctors (PhD) themselves need to come down on survey. The analogy is we need MA (Medical Assistant) more than physician (Medical Doctor).

When Dr Mahathir starts on industrial vision, he starts 'less in degree graduate and less in non-skill workers, but more in diploma level'.

6.5.4 - FODDER FACTORY

It is still on R&D, I deeply willingness to do this. Any researcher should try this because the impact is extremely big for the country. Please see 'the cows and cross country'. You just imagine if the cows industries is in a confinement[189] like chicken industries. The grass will feed rather than cross country. This is not new as Peter Ryan of Australia did it since 1990's or earlier. He faces a lot of problem since they are 4 seasons. He had to canvas for climates control using air conditioner, heater, blower and definitely microcontroller[190]. In Malaysia we only need a shelter and irrigation system no need a lot of thing. It can be open air, no heater, blower and air conditioner[191]. The weather is likely constant all over the year.

The main research is the cow and the fodder itself. In Australia, Peter Ryan had barley and oat for seeding. Is Malaysian paddy or green peas (sprout) or anything can be taken? What the cost like, the supply of seed and so on. Beside that what the growth like. How many kilograms against the amount of fodder and also the period of taken.

I had an idea on the analysis. Firstly let 3 or 4 cattle to be analysing to confine on the weight bridge all the time. I can design the weight bridge. Now a day all load cells (under platform) digitise able and very easy. So you can have real time record, convert it and send wireless, even throughout the world[192].

Microcontroller like in this picture has to design – custom made.

---

[189] This is what Bernard (see 6.6.3 – Economic segregation) design in Netherland. Semi-automatic system needs not a farmer to see their cattle for two or three weeks. Feeding up to ploughing the faeces out will be done by the system automatically.

[190] Complexity in design of microcontroller will be much more many folds than what we need for Malaysia.

[191] Electrical design much more simple, power consumption very much lower.

[192] It is good for Malaysian overseas student to do research Malaysia-abroad simultaneously let say with 4 season Australian cattle's comparison in the same particular year.

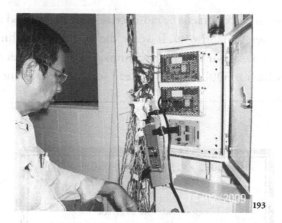

193

Software can record most of the thing day by day. Time and the weight of fodder feed, photograph, and the 'waste' out and so on.

Current weight	(n+δ) kg.
Initial weight	(n) kg.
Weight gain	(δ) kg.
Period of feeding	(d) days
fodder	(w) kg.
Total cost of fodder	RM (M)
Weight rated (weight of fodder/weight gain)	(w/δ)
Cost rated (Fodder cost/weight gain)	(M/δ) RM/kg.
… and so on …	

6.5.5 - TECHNICAL IDEAS

Due to my experience Malaysian technocrats always have many ideas. Unfortunately they always had been supress by higher clans who is too much worries about their position and so on.

For example I had an idea as above (as to UMP) – 'Industri Padi' (Paddy Industry). I spread it easily with no restriction.

That one consider easy (but very high impact to the country) because it dealing with heavy machinery. It visible and touchable compare to with bacteria,

---

193   This is my complete Design & Build – Light conveyor system (horizontal move then vertical down to lower floor) **Microcontroller card and its programming done by another Malay folk, 2009, Pasir Gudang Johor

viruses, microorganism or nucleus or radioactive talk. Visible and touchable is easy to work together even to hand-over. It won't 'die' easily. If you think problem with heavy machinery, how about very high technology oil and gas let say in North Sea or Terengganu which is 300km away in deep sea and how about this?

```
┌─────────────────────────────────────────┐
│                                         │
│        J062 - PERMISSION PENDING        │
│        ─────────────────────            │
│                                         │
│         Utusan Malaysia 2/11/2005       │
│   Article and windmill photo – North Philippine │
│                                         │
└─────────────────────────────────────────┘
```

194

It is windmills in North Philippine. It is current technology RE, 15 set very high precision, giant mechanical movement as high as 23 storey building, heavy construction works due to each nacelle (base / footing) is bring up to 100 tons weight. 'Risk' calculation is considerable high due to hurricane dynamic region and some more the constructor is from Denmark.

Let surf this;

http://www.everbluetraining.com/blog/nature-wind-farms

Now let see how big these windmills - onshore, near-shore & offshore. It is about same in Philippine. Each blade is about 12 tons and as high as 25 storey building

Please go to;

https://www.google.com/search?q=windmill+northwich&ie=utf-8&oe=utf-8#q=wind+energy

Then, go to;

'Images for wind energy' or 'More images for wind energy'

Now we can imagine how big and how many the windmills are.

---

194   News, UM 2 Nov, 2005, Electric Windmill

It is nothing at all, you not even to raise a head, my design is just primitive technology 100meter girder[195]; it is only about 35 ton. If you put load about 5 ton, it's only 40 tons in total. Divide for 2 tractors (as prime mover) its only 20 tons each. We had dynamic axle pivot for trailer up to more than 70 tons each just to be engineered in KL only, maybe somewhere in Sungai Buluh. Local fabricator design a jacket, transport, offload and lower down and stand up on sea-bed without big problem

In this kind of small case I had no worry at all because I mostly like to be **all in one** and I have long hand to acquire a help on higher thing. I personally easy to communicate (in all aspect of related engineering Mechanical, Electrical, Electronics, ICT / software and especially in Instrumentation which is less people in it) with any new person.

As what I claim is like this;

I'm consultant, I'm engineer, I'm technician, I'm foreman, I'm designer, I'm draftsman, I'm office boy, I'm clerk, I'm supervisor, I'm QC, I'm negotiator to hardware, I'm welder, I'm lorry driver, I'm porter, I'm wash man, I'm cleaning man & I'm also bouncer to protect the work.

The following 'Precision Farming' / 'Precision Agriculture', all in all will be rationalise by technocrats who become a farmers together with traditional farmers.

---

[195] Talk about 100 meter; from that internet surfing, there are some of 100 sets of wind turbines per project in deep sea, their high are about 25 storey building just above the water surface alone.

[196] You can see from this model how an oil rig look like, photo taken in Universiti Teknologi Petronas, Perak on May 26, 2003. Note, this model is Duyong Complex it is about 300km Terengganu offshore

By that time the integration of ideas (farmers and technocrat) we can see a lot of strange machines (maybe some like rainbow) to be run in the field. It is not impossible the emerging of idea to integrate all small lot become bigger for easy to manages by using big machines or equipment.

6.5.5.1 - Precision Agriculture

The Malaysian farming should start wherever necessary to integrate small land plot to become 'economical' scale in size. There are a lot in Malays hand. That is starting of everything as the entire problem will stuck here. How to start is another problem.

From there then only move to the current technologies for example 'precision agriculture'. In this topic I would like to draw attention to these 3 overviews as some sort like 'introduction'.

Please run through these entire webs.

By: PRT 2008; UPM, Malaysia: Agriculture and Man

http://www.slideshare.net/mandalina/precision-agriculture?related=2

Precision agriculture on the Northern Plain John Nowatzki North Dakota State University - overview

http://www.slideshare.net/JohnNowatzki/precision-agriculture-an-overview?related=3

This slideshare quite long but the first slide is enough to get an idea.

http://www.slideshare.net/sduttarganvi/realtime-nitrogen-management-in-rice?related=3

Still not clear what the precision agriculture is?

I thought this IBM RESEARCH article quite useful.

http://www.research.ibm.com/articles/precision_agriculture.shtml

For IBM researcher and Distinguished Engineer Ulisses Mello and a team of scientists from IBM Research – Brazil, the answer to that daunting (food supply to feed world by 2050) challenge lies in real time data gathering and analysis. They are researching how "precision agriculture" techniques and technologies can maximize food production, minimize environmental impact and reduce cost.

Traditionally agriculture is practiced by performing a particular task, such as planting or harvesting, against a predetermined schedule. But by collecting real-time data on weather, soil and air quality, crop maturity and even equipment and labor costs and availability, predictive analytics can be used to make smarter decisions. This is known as precision agriculture.

Still in elaboration of this article don't forget to run through about 'Deep Thunder and Precision Agriculture' by Lloyd Treinish Chief Scientist - Deep Thunder,

https://youtu.be/qVn9FOnRSHg

That is considering as the main principle / idea / point of view / an eminent peak. The high efficiency in food production is priority.

If 'economical size' of land plots was achieved everything likes to goes well and we can see next step. Then please consider these.

https://www.youtube.com/watch?v=IpcG9nAYWL8
Farmers reap benefits of driverless tractor tech
Self-driving tractor; Bondurant, IOWA
This is not important at the moment but the idea will tell us how far we can go.

Next, a lot of thing but it is too far from main issue for this book. Everybody is freely to surf these entire web.
For all Muslim, this is not provocative or anything just the matter of knowledge as what we know Israel also had a lot of top management books in the world to choose from.

https://www.youtube.com/watch?v=oxxYmn3HpDU&ebc=ANyPxKpN_
573cL3nD_UlbLuN7JQh2VifZtcRgERtUMP-4RY7DjLgI2x09L731kP_
gwgiTfXx_HBUOtF_NkJzfEjVXMgzP3mN8g
@ Made in Israel; Agriculture.

https://www.youtube.com/watch?v=28DNuMQCi3Y&ebc=ANyPxKrzn
E0Fp7_glYsOt86do9L6pnotiPdUYnFK3PXY56QVAoOUYUJmlg08kzgLS_
MDLgdmMhHUxNpuAtNRlzUD70wOylkkjA
@ Amazing agriculture technology, deutz fahr tractor collection, farm tractor equipment

https://www.youtube.com/watch?v=PLI_50RXBiE

@ Amazing agriculture machine compilation, crazy farm tractor, new technology farming

**The first machine in this compilation, let see how potatoes small machine harvesting.

https://www.youtube.com/watch?v=L52MnXLTk3c

@ World's Mini Agricultural machinery;

Mini corn combine harvester, spray fertilizer - rice, sugar cane from Thailand' www.sakpattana.com

When we talk about precision agriculture *'Universiti Putra Malaysia'* (UPM) with a few various agencies including MACRES (Malaysia Remote Sensing) endeavour to make this run through. Thanks for their effort and successful. But I have 'sense' something difference especially in Kedah. UPM 'study camp' was in Tanjung Karang Selangor.

Malaysian National Paddy Precision Farming Project

http://www.apan.net/meetings/kualalumpur2009/proposals/Agriculture/ APAN%20Eb%20Edit.pdf

Then I propose *'Industri Padi'* (Paddy Industries) to various places including to Prime Minister and *'Universiti Malaysia Pahang'*.

I was born and during childhood, young period just within paddy planting life in Kedah. I used to do all about paddy just manually, by buffalo or by bicycle only. In 2004 after 30 years in Klang Valley I back again to Kedah for five years.

It is too much changes and I become stranger. There are a lot of stupid problem in paddy industries especially gangsterism[197] and uneconomical size of land plot due to inheritance.

I gather with farmers and follow closely for the years then I proposed[198].

---

[197] For example; you had no choice to bring any harvesting machine to your plot because yours is belong to certain gang territory, must through them. They will decide. Another area is irrigation problem, the water had through the neighbour plot. Synchronization is not easy and to the detriment in every aspect especially time and economic factors.

[198] I cannot attach the write-up, quantitative analysis and numerical facts here due to not make longer discussion and bore for non-interested party. Later to be contact if there any interested party.

In certain point of view we had difference type of soil condition, cannot simply copy from outside and bring certain heavy machinery in. Moreover the outside cultivation most on dry land. Never underestimate![199]

For example, now the soil conditions become deeper and worsening. The efficiency of the whole must be affected due to wasting of everything for example, heavy tractor stuck on for a week, to overcome over depth as the soil become highly liquidate sludge by those heavy machineries

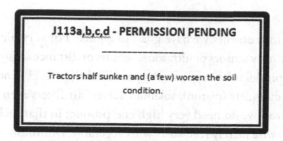

J113a,b,c,d - PERMISSION PENDING

Tractors half sunken and (a few) worsen the soil condition.

200

If one follows my proposal it is outstanding (the local need). It was 'aerial operated'. You are lowering down aeroplane (fertilizer spreader) to the earth.

The most important is to vanish unnecessary 'bull power' of laborers which now too much depend on foreigner especially Bangladesh and Thailand.

---

[199] As HSBC (the world's local bank) – Never underestimate the importance of local knowledge. To truly understand a country and it culture, you have to be part of it.

[200] All this 4- 2014, My Kedah local clan collection. The readers can surf in internet 'Tractor wheely'

This will change the scenario as you are in safety boots to work in paddy plantation rather than now with bare foot to walk in paddy field.

Final stage of my architectural / design will be the girder and both prime mover [201] works like as plotter (printers) on your office desk. It is wireless from control room with the support of control mast[202] cum as communication tower (maybe), surveillance sensor to plant enemy and maybe viewing platform or 'real' high-tea discussion table at 15 meters above ground level.

As my proposal to be design and fabricate locally from a to z it will cost effective i.e only about 20 or 30 percent from offered price of any highly professional body. We need not to sub out in total. We orchestrate the whole thing[203]. The vendors only need to supply if maximum up to 'living room and not in bedroom'. They only provide us the 'prescription' of their products. The rest is ours. For control mast or viewing tower just need to use spotlight mast in local, let say 'Galvapoles' brand.

Let say for instruments we have great of choice. For very high precision and critical like proximity sensors or ultrasonic sensors or distance sensors we can choose from high end products let say P+F (Pepperl+Fuchs) or E+H (Endress+Hauser).

But for air cylinders (piston), solenoid valves, air filters even gauges (just for standing indicator) we no need very high end product in that such kind of robust condition, otherwise merely feed cows with vegetable. Multitasking and very high precision instrument are just use to indicate the existence of air.

It is quiet common, if I on professional design I must adopt high quality equipment in order to make myself as far as possible away from any defect to protect enough reputation and land me to comfortable sleep.

---

[201]   Prime-mover - Tractors in my current design

[202]   (with independence solar powered equipment)

[203]   The previous experience is shows that outside design (i.e. Japan) always not exactly meet the local problem. That why a lot of modification made for the most of the machines. Indirectly it is shows 'village engineers' had creativity and another thing the problem just solve for time being before new problem arise. As I heard from an old man before "today problem will replace with new problem tomorrow, lively. Even pesticide and weed killer are cannot be same as a few years back (some sort like virus in computer – progressively changing). Natural enemy also changing"

6.6 - Tanjung Pagar, Singapore

Tanjung Pagar; is gone case on 27 June, 2011 without any good return to Malaysia.

```
J068 - PERMISSION PENDING
─────────────────
Harian Metro 21/1/2012
KL-S'pore; Tanjung Pagar
Photo: Najib & Lee Hsien Loong
```

204

Congratulation to Singapore, you are very clever. Then you can overcome a hell lot of problem easily. You are tremendously better than Jews of Palestine. No bloodshed.

6.6.1 - HIGH RANGE - VEGETABLES FED COWS

How much the damage (production) cost for each entire job. Is Malaysian stupid?

205
,

206
,

204 News, HM 21 Jan 2012, KL-Singapore
205 ZP's, Nov 2010, Nenasi Pekan
206 ZP's, Nov 2010, Klang

 207,

 208,

 209,

 210,

 211

 212,

---

207   ZP's, Apr 2012, Kuantan

208   ZP's, Oct,2012, Pasir Gudang

209   ZP's, Apr, 2013, Pekan

210   ZP's, Oct,2012, Pasir Gudang

211   ZP's, Mac, 2014, Kuantan

212   ZP's, Jan 2011, Pekan

213 ZP's, Jun 2013, Rompin
214 ZP's, May 2014, Nenasi
215 ZP's, Jan 2012, Pasir Gudang
216 ZP's, Jan,2012, Endau Johore
217 ZP's, Oct 25,2012, Pasir Gudang
218 ZP's, Nov, 2011,Pekan

219 ZP's, May,2014, Kuantan
220 ZP's, Dec,12,2012, Pekan
221 ZP's, Nov,2011, Pekan
222 ZP's, Feb,2011, Tiram, Johor.
223 ZP's, April,2011,Nenasi
224 ZP's, April,2011,Nenasi

225 , 226 .

Those are the Malaysian scenario.

It weird for normal people to feed cows with green vegetable isn't it? That is my analogy to that scenario. It is expensive. They will be very far behind and lose competitiveness to Vietnam and Thailand in no time.

Actually Malaysian Chinese were ready to make a move to make very special museum and showcase for all Malays (as what the Malay want). Maybe National Palace is the right place.

Sorry to all Sultans. The first class traitor is around. The culprit wants all the sultans to be outcast together with all Malay. Historical mean simply just repeat, everybody can see Singapore Malay sultanate is over. Land plot (maybe last piece) of palace was acquire in this paper cutting.

J083a - PERMISSION PENDING

Berita Harian 29/5/1999
S'pore offer RM44,400 to Sultan Hussein's inheritors to clear 160 years Kampong Glam Palace

J083b - PERMISSION PENDING

Berita Harian 29/5/1999
S'pore offer – continuing pages

227 , 228 .

---

225 ZP's,2014,Nenasi
226 ZP's, July,2014, Nenasi
227 News, Berita Harian, May 29,1999
228 Ibid (continuing)

Malaysian Malays should ready now to be in showcase. Nothing is wrong isn't it?

It is the MALAY OUTCAST

Just to think, why not Malaysian agriculture use Rolls-Royce to haul the manure (fertilizer of animal waste) to the farm. Its bonnets and car itself is big. Moreover it comforts. It will be world record. For RR Ghost, Government will get RM 54,502 for annual road-tax. Slightly larger RR Phantom he will get RM 56,621.50 per year. It mean about RM 1,000 a week. Wow … It's not big problem by selling a papaya or a bunch of banana at RM 1,000, sure can pay (road-tax only). If 1 million farmers had one each, its mean government revenue is about Ringgit Malaysia 1 billion of road-tax bills per week. Real great! It's now for new tag of version 2 another 1MDB.

Yeah! … … this Ghost bolehhh … …

The Trailers:

- **By Tractor**

How about this? It's big yet powerful enough for certain purpose, but it slow, very limited usage and distance and nuisance for road use.

229

Somehow rather it is not attractive to the youth. It's just practical in the farm.

---

229   ZP's, Nov,2013,Nenasi

- **By a car**

This '*kampung*' engineer's car trailer is properly done but not certified still illegal mean.

- **By a motorcycle**

This '*kampong*' engineer's motorcycle trailer is properly done but definitely cannot for the road use. There some peoples have to use it for survival with some big reasons. So we already encourage our people to do wrong thing – cheat to government and law.

6.6.2 - THE LOWER RANGE - CRACKPOT …

Slightly lower range you can see this activities. It also depends on time and the places where they are.

---

230   ZP's, Mac,2015, Nenasi
231   ZP's, Mac,2015,Nenasi

232,
233,
234,
235,
236,
237,

232 ZP's, July,2011,Sijangkang
233 ZP's, July,2011,Sijangkang
234 ZP's, Aug,2011,Klang
235 ZP's, Feb,2011,Nenasi
236 ZP's, Aug,2011,Sijangkang
237 ZP's, Aug,2011,Sijangkang

238,
239,
240,
241,
242,

238 ZP's, May 2012,Putat Kedah
239 ZP's,2014,Nenasi
240 ZP's, July 2014,Nenasi
241 ZP's, Dec 2013,Nenasi
242 ZP's, Dec 2013,Pekan

Do we are thinking all those fellows are some sort of crackpot? They don't know what is the proper carrier for their goods?

Yes good! … the proper carrier cannot service them. They know just with a stupid calculation, they cannot afford any pretty wife which their cosmetics alone will carry about RM 2,900/ month since their income just exactly RM 3,000.

---

243   ZP's, May 2014,Nenasi

244   ZP's, July 2011,Nenasi

245   ZP's, Dec 2013,Jitra

246   ZP's, Dec 2014,Perlis

247   ZP's, Jun 2014,Nenasi

Haa ... there are ...
The WORLD RECORD ...
In Malaysia, you need to be rich before you can become poor farmer.

6.6.3 - ECONOMIC SEGREGATION (BY OUTSIDERS' OPINION)

This couple Bernard & Thea are from Amsterdam.

,

,

,

The pictures were taken in house and outside my house at Angullia Resort, Pekan, Pahang, August 2010.

It is more than one year they cycle before arrive to my house. Last destination is New Zealand expecting total will be 1 ½ year.

---

248 All 4 – Aug,2010,Nenasi, Pekan

They are spending with budget of about Euro 120 per day and simply difference with no rushing. They will enjoy a few days sometimes 2 weeks to every place they stop. It would be hotel and resorts. In Malaysia they more or less like Hotel Sri Malaysia.

I had frequently asked his opinion about Malaysia. He reluctant just quotes good, very good, nice country and so on.

Actually I like to see from economic perspective but then he still reluctant. Finally "To be frank, I just want to know only. No obligation nothing." Only then he brief through his journey it is very big flaw in Malaysian society. Very contrast between big bungalow in next to almost collapse house and this is quite common along the road.

If you travel around you can see this colourful of absurdity.

During Dr Mahathir time, this Italian, Scabbury (electrical electronic engineering trainer / didactic, De Lorenzo of Italy) came and also had been asked. The comment is logic and positive. His sincerity and the reason made can be seeing subject to surrounding as he follows me to many places like Melaka, Johor, Pahang, Terengganu and mainly Selangor (including some villages).

Here some pictures

And so with this Swedish, Per Erik Olson – Geophysical instrument, ABEM of Sweden.

250   ZP's, June 2002, Melaka, KUTKM (now Universiti Teknikal),
251   ZP's, June 2002, Karak (on the way back from Terengganu and Pahang),
252   ZP's, June 2002, KLCC (Petronas Twin Tower),
253   ZP's, Sept 2002, Sijangkang (quite big village Klang remote)

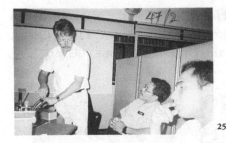 

254, 255

There is a lot more to say. Like this one, Toni from city of love (Paris) together with Dr Bashir of Uniten (Universiti Tenaga Nasional)(regarding Staubli robot arm); it was about credit to Dr Mahathir and Malaysia. He had been asked about his Proton Perdana V6 (WHW ....). He thumbs up both hands and shake a head. 'Very good car'

256

---

254   ZP's, Feb 2002,Ipoh (IPG- Geology Research Institute)
255   ZP's, Feb 2002,KL [JPS(Department of Irrigation)]
256   All 3 – ZP's, Mac 2002, Uniten, Kajang.

6.6.4 - CEO

How to Think Like A CEO – D.A.Benton; Warner Books; Page 409;

A big mistake a CEO makes is to hire people he feels comfortable with. That isn't what he needs. Look for people who can do the job best, even if you don't get along. My CFO never supported me on anything. He was honest and kept the book right. And he pointed out all of my mistakes. He really made me think. You're not going to have growth if everybody is thinking the same.

-Ernie Howell

Retired President,

Packaging Systems International (D.A.Benton, 1999, p. 409).

Are the Malay leaders thinks all the international big industries are stupid spending to hire QC as their work some sort like villain? There are quiet common quarrels or fighting between QC and Production department. For the Malay management, simply wipe off QC Department it will settle the problem and save the cost and straight into their personal account.

Most likely the Malay leader are predispose to be a villain who force drives their clan to the graves.

6.6.5 - TRANSFORMATION

Transformation for all.

J107a - PERMISSION PENDING

Harian Metro 20/3/2013
Transformation for all – token cash (BR1M); income rise
to 5k; poverty reduce to 1.7%; criminal down 27%

257

The great confusing look like upside down.

---

257 News, Harian Metro, Mac 20,2013

Whatever means positive it is negative and vice versa.

Increase in income for RM5,000 is questionable? It is self-dissenting by giving token cash of BR1M to citizen.

,

,

,

,

,

,

258

259

6.6.6 - 'SUARA BARU' (THE CURRENT VOICES)

This one I bought in small town, Muara in Brunei in November 2008.

```
┌─────────────────────────────────────────┐
│                                         │
│      J108a - PERMISSION PENDING         │
│                                         │
│      ─────────────────                  │
│                                         │
│       'Suara Baru' – November 2008      │
│  The magazine that time talk mainly about how the Malay │
│        is going to be in the hand of Najib │
│                                         │
└─────────────────────────────────────────┘
```

---

258 All 7 – ZP's,(2010 -2015),Pekan
259 ZP's,2012, Masai Johor

So it mean Brunei Malay also follow Malaysian Malay.

Under subtitle 'Naxxx Era'

"Is he capable to bring new hope or just to complete last breath of UMNO?"

J108b - PERMISSION PENDING

'Suara Baru' – November 2008
Editorial – Anuar Mohd Nor talking about rehabilitation
of UMNO in Najib's hand, is it posibble?

From the comment of the editor Anuar Mohd Noor since 2008 he already can smell a rat. But the good person like him always positive thinking and hoping good.

Chapter 3
No Tea No Coffee

PART 7.0 - NO TEA NO COFFEE

7.1 - Sabirin
(From Prologue/coffee shop)

News BH16/03/09 – Astronautical *(ATSB, pelopor industri teknologi angkasa)*

7.2 - Inflation

(From 5.2.1)

Uncontrollable inflation was created by the latest two prime ministers in order to influence bureaucrat votes.

It is derives from the word inflate.

If you want to inflate your bicycle tyre (or any tyre) you will inflate gradually with considerate manner. Simply rush up you will know what will happen.

I am in position not to talk about this. But generally by thinking you can analyse and summarise in simple meaning.

I personally had experience with Chinese educated Malay. Most of his business friends are Chinese. He is fluent in major Chinese dialect. Let his name is Mr Saiman.

I need to borrow his engineering workers and to pay directly. I am very lucky because his workers really committed to the job and I finish very much earlier.

The section of one week budgeting time they just finish within a few hours and I consider as one day. I save a lot in time, workers, machinery, transport and all miscellaneous.

To cut short, after the job finish he asks how much I want to pay.

I said I want to pay RM40.00 (per day). The standard rate is just RM20.00 that time.

He straight stand-up and start his 'lecture'

"No,no,no......don't ever do that. Simply pay as what I did. It is lucky I ask. By hook or by crook they only need their salary RM20.00. Whether the job is success is not important to them. So you cannot share your profit with them because they also don't want to share when you are losing. This is standard law. That losing time you will cover with this profit".

He continue, "That is not very important, the most important is you destroy everything. You destroy me; destroy them and even you yourselves. You understand me?

This is the Chinese education I had. Most of my business friends are Chinese.

When you start giving them I will be the first victim, by comparing, they will start ask every time and it became their new salary. When it start go up it will never come down. It is quite clear?"

"You listen! If they have to come back to you again, do you thing they will not dream that much? Definitely so. For them it doesn't matter whether you get good price or not for this new project. They will say last time RM40.00". That is standard.

"This is 'inflation' and to be control. It is like spending. You control the 'inflate' by not giving at all or by giving one dollar, by one dollar you and them will can live longer (time). If you 'spending' five dollars, by five dollars or ten dollars you will have no more 'room' and your life as well their life will be shorter. Which one is better?

You no need to request for your dead, sooner or later it surely come. So, as long as possible you elongate your life span.

If you really need to give them, it should be in term of bonus or allowance, that's unlimited and it will not reflect in salary in future. No commitment as what salary need".

It's doesn't matter if you want to give one thousand or ten even a million. They know in their mind, this is just one-off. So please don't spoil or destroy their mind. It means in future if not RM40 they cannot work since their productivity is unparalleled.

Now we can see how the Chinese way of thinking (even low level in society) – very far beyond imagination even to the Malay top leaders.

What is this?

Like this if PM inflate bureaucrat salary scale again in order to overcome the situation, let say who ever getting salary now is four thousand inflate to twenty thousand, it will solve problem for short while only since the country burden is unrealistic. Then what happen to the country that time? It is chaotic and going to bankrupt? That is what Mr Saiman said, 'your life span become shorter'. The Malay will be outcast too fast. Don't put a brain in arse to shit out.

'But the Malays have apparently learnt nothing from the near loss of their country in the past'[260].

Somehow rather it is never mind because there had Singapore Lee Hsien Loong and Lim Guan Eng (which not even need Datukship or Tan Sri) to take care the entire stray cats and stray dogs after they shit-out their own country. They never think about their next generation will widdle (pee) on their graves.

---

[260] Dr Mahathir: Jan 24, 2008 by Dinobeano

This part (inflation) is impairment and will take long time to recover unless to be done by a good leader.

7.2.1 - ZERO INFLATION

No inflation at all maybe we can say zero inflation and the mutual, stable and balance increment is same thing. I am not in position to talk about this even this is coffee shop or *'warung'* (coffee stall) session.

Everybody was invited and try to understand as what Dr Mahathir says about this.

You can visit (Jomo, 2010, p. 168)

He excerpt from 'Vision 2020: The Way Forward' of Mahathir full speech in the congress on 29 April, 1997.

That time, after six years the vision is on track a lot of countries were study and simulate that vision for their own.

From Botswana to El Salvador, Colombia to Nigeria, Mauritius to Venezuela were decided their own vision 2020, Rome club want it for Europe, so ASEAN and APEC.

What happen to the country now is economy cripple down due to wildness inflate of bureaucrats[261] wages in order to persuade strong support to government. It is too much politicking rather than fundamental business life consideration. In the Malay old folks they said *'tong kosong'*[262]. Shout and shout everywhere but nobody wants to listen.

You can give how much you want but the impact is very bad. Consider you give super bike to 18 years old boy just after his driving licence acquired. You will not teach him an endurance life. Definitely he will happy but it is not comparable. It won't last, end up he will ask more without appreciation. Worse thing he might easily involve in severe accident.

---

[261]   Edward Heath (Britain) lose in election since too much depend on bureaucrat (Mastika, 1974, p. 73)
[262]   *'Tong Kosong'* it mean 'empty tank'. The sound is big but nothing inside.

The senior must control[263] sub-ordinate. Parent must control the children and leader must control the country situation.

It is common to see a lot of civil servant having expensive car not comparable to them. Once they sign for nine years loan, it cannot retract back because total liability is very high[264] to withdraw because their early commitment to the goods is zero (zero down payment).

A long the way they carry the goods (cars) there a lot of trouble some. Some periodically and some uncertainty end up on the fifth every month all the money were spend out and worse for not enough. But the fact the salary is not low as what that two PM gifted.

All of all this will led them to a part time job. It is very wrong doing. But it is weird to see that two PM encourage and campaign to do so.

One of the famous Shaw Organisation movies (in Merdeka Film)[265] shows how bad the practice is.

It is the teacher is always sleeping in the class because at the same time he works at night club.

The question is how needing a teachers of nine or ten years old students to drive Rolls, Jaguar, Range Rover, Pontiac or Cadillac to school? Moreover it is plus driver or straight by chopper (helicopter).

For this kind of thing they should go for business and not as teacher. Nothing is wrong. It is appropriate. When you merge together, we can see so many of them have to put priority on his part time business because he no need to worry about his 'non disturb' salary.

Anything is over than normal is weird look and no good. Whether over-acting, over-kill, over spending, over-stay and most of the thing.

---

263   Control – for example, last a few decades, to purchase a car we need to put maybe 50% as down-payment. So we had some tangible value on the goods not like now, no control for zero down payments, and worse false inflated wages slip - maximum full liability. Without control is what we see now in Malaysia, especially Malay vulnerable to bankrupts.

264   Total liability is very high maybe more than double plus all side payment and fees.

265   The title 'Masam-masam Manis' directed by P.Ramlee

7.3 - Lim Kheng Yaik

(From Prolog – outside in)

```
┌─────────────────────────────────────┐
│  J112 - PERMISSION PENDING           │
│  ─────────────────────               │
│                                      │
│      Berita Harian 26/7/2005         │
│  The Malay leaders must more rational: Kheng Yaik │
│        (A Chinese minister)          │
└─────────────────────────────────────┘
```

News BH 26/07/2005 The Malay leader should be more rational – Kheng Yaik

7.4 - 'Syariah' Court

(from 2.2.1.3.1.)

If we look higher up syariahsome *'syariah'* court[266] lawyers' just petty fogger and some judges will sell their dignity to the dog. How much? Yeah… as low as three thousand dollars they simply booked one of the hell's 'genuine key'.

What they learn in universities? Maybe how to create easy money by riding on Islamic law practising and repent later? They know when to die?

Unfortunately there was nothing to hinder them. Pity them, everything run smoothly to the hell because they are undoubtedly holding the Islamic flag along their way.

There are some of those petty foggers are chasing to be politician. It is easy to understand, for extra easier room to plunder and definitely in UMNO, the most top unlimited corrupted party. It can go as low as two or three dollars until multi billion dollars; from lowest grade officer until the most top – all covered, lock stock and barrels. Malaysia?.......+ their mothers were sold-out!!

---

[266] *'Syariah court'* it mean Islamic legislation court of justice

To believe, suppose the most top secure, jet fighter engines in Malaysia arm forces can be stolen. We are talking about engine only not the whole. Just imagine!

It is lucky maybe just for time being only, one of them (petty foggers) already loose in his try in Selangor in last general election.

The record shows his 'golden touch' will like razor blade. His cooperative with judge will land him in real success. It doesn't matter how stupid and loose the cases is.

Let say the police report stamped shows it forbidden use in court, they still use and consider part of their strong evidence. The point and content are not important at all. The important is just a piece of paper of police report for show. Childish, child's play baby doll! The court is just a playground.

So with medical report; nothing shows, everything is in good, comfortable, fair, no bruise, no haemorrhage, intact but the important is 'a piece of medical report'. Worse thing, for example medical report shows the patient father's name is wrong (for example, Salim to be writing as Salleh. It's very different meaning at all), wrong ages, without I/C number. It is look like the doctor professionally and purposely makes in order to avoid 'involvement' in injustice because she also Muslim.

What kind a court of justice they are?

- They simply ignore the very basic principle and the essence of justice just because of 'their baby dolls concealed in their playground' and nobody can see.
- They can go prosecution without a concrete case on any individual?
- They should remember that the correct policy in relation to prosecution is that there must be no doubt at all (reasonable doubt) before a person is charged. Just balance of probability cannot be accepted even how bad the case is.
- For the above case is straight forward. The most laziest and stupid judge, with half eyes open still knows that is gone case and should be dropped. No head-ache at all.

So the problem is bribery.
Justification;

- The judge supposes need not to worry, either plaintiff or defendant win.
- The judge needs to see 'fighting' and not join in and to be sided to any party.

- How come the judge and plaintiff's lawyer stood up like gangster to punch defendant in proceeding[267] which was call earlier to be push to the end of session so that no public watch. Why both of them cowardly don't response immediately to fight outside of the court building ('their own ground') as requested by defendant in that proceeding itself.

If any defendant try to defence, straight away warning to charge 'contempt of court'. It is really one way single full of power, behind the scene.

It is too obvious; then there had some defendants dare to 'fight' for themself without having any lawyer and ignore about consequences.

There one case[268] the defendant was charge mad due to his affidavit and the court order was issued.

What the funny is, in the court order there is the word *'memerintahkan[269]'* and *'mendapatkan rawatan[270]* in Psychiatric Unit in General Hospital Kuala Lumpur and without any letter 'from the court to hospital'.

The 'patient' needs just to bring court order. It is real funny.

Psychiatric Unit (as what the judge refer) in their response, "you cannot simply jump here, must come through psychiatrist. We don't know anything about court order; you must register at counter and run through all the procedures."

There a lot of hassles at hospital counter as they cannot act against that kind of letter. After briefing from 'patient', finally all of them conclude he must see medical officer (doctor) first. Before that there is a big surprise when they ask where the patient now and the 'patient' said he himself.

In consultation room one more thing happen; non-Muslim (Sikh) physician (doctor) calls so many staff to gathering to be witness maybe.

With humble and polite, "I don't know about Islamic court; I as medical officer it mean doctor, the man like you[271], if I simply write *please refer to psychiatric*, just like that, it is a lot of big things there. First I must responsible. Secondly if you kill somebody, that guy is freely died. It is another thing if you are lucky, you can be rich man in another court case".

---

267 MAL BIL: 481/98 (SA);Mahkamah Rendah Syariah Daerah Petaling, Selangor
268 MAL BIL: 1342-40-4/99; (Court Order) Mahkamah Rendah Syariah Daerah Petaling, Selangor
269 It mean 'instructed or ordered'
270 It mean 'to get treatment' – suppose 'assessment' only. The judge tries to overcome psychiatrist job.
271 Nothing shows any indication to refer to psychiatric.

The doctor continue, "It should start with assessment and doctor's discretion to refer higher. 'To get treatment[272]' is very strong word and very danger for misappropriates by doctor.

That is how stupid they are. When you become '*Syariah court judge*', you are so big[273]. All over the world is under your instruction, including doctors and psychiatrics in hospital.

That is how bad perception to Islam just by the hands of their trusted men. Nothing wrong to the outsiders' interpretation, that is 'the truth'.

No wonder a lot of humiliate grumble, '*Syariah*'court just a 'court in mosquitos-net' or 'court of cocks and fanny (genitalia)'.

Then what happen?

The 'patient' was founded not mad, now he is back to be a 'defendant' again. Along with him is a 'special dictation' on a clinic card. He acquires a 'certificate' with very powerful 'weapon' now.

He was eager waiting for next proceeding.

Then he continues, this time with more confidence and bombastic end up with an expected 'contempt of court' and trail out to prison. He had been offered to request forgiveness but he declined.

Unfortunately for the authority they had to call the press for their publicity but the mishap bounce back to them as the journalists wrote distinctly with 95% truth of every step monitoring which is much more credited to defendant and worse it is reflect to their own stupidity.

The front page, very bad headline[274] was '*Hina Hakim Syaitan*'[275]. It is true assumption by journalists as anybody who follows the proceeding will be the same. They must be clever enough to choose headline and expression.

On the midst of proceeding the judge was realise the case had never 'mention[276]' and express out his anger to defendant but not his problem.

Silently the defendant thought, this is another bomb is waiting for.

---

272   In the actual words (in Malay) in court order is '*mendapatkan rawatan*'.
273   Actually in Islamic faith, it is reversely and distinctly stated, one of two feet, of two of three judges is already in the hell. To show how care should be taken.
274   News, Harian Metro 2 Feb, 2000. Please forward to 7.9 – Hina Hakim Syaitan (but a Malay newspaper)
275   '*Hina Hakim Syaitan*' it mean Insulting of Satanic Judge
276   This was happen because they are too greedy for 'another packet of corruption' by creating new task, very loose contempt of court after glance through affidavit. Not a problem at all for them.

After out of the jail[277] he had received the 'original copy' of notice for 'mention' date[278].

He was thinking wildly,

Firstly;... "What the hell of this Islamic court?"

The prime (1st level) case never mentions much less a proceeding,

(Analogy -Not even married, not even making a child yet)

He had been charge contempt of court[279] (suppose a 2nd level),

He was committed to the jail and complete course for this derivative case.

(Analogy – he already 'awarded' grandson grow-up and could run)

Secondly; it is so wicked, they are very 'expert' in handling of misconduct and all of bad practices but then they still missing one. They are so smart supposed to make back-dated of the document and keep in their file. Defendant just victim and cannot do anything, so many related documents they decline to give. Later when defendant request a copy of court order to jail the judge simply decline and said, "Cannot, after you will manipulate"

It weird isn't it? The defendant could manipulate judge, lawyer and court? After they get caught on their own bobby trap[280]?

That is how many steps they jump over.

Now he needs to be backward, 'start all over again?' jail again?

He thought again, they were creating their own bobby trap. Articles 125 Federal Constitution will show no absolute immunity to the judges. Due to misconduct under tribunal they still can be charge.

Never mind, it is too far beyond redemption. Defendant, eureka! There should be havoc and chaotic throughout the country through Islamic bodies of individual states plus a lot of other Islamic movement institutions inclusive universities, colleges, mosques and *'surau'*. Booklets, pamphlets and soft copy CD's distributed vastly.

What the issue?

'Illegitimate sexual first then only to be married is not an offence (if you can pay) under Islamic Dept. of Selangor (JAIS)'

---

277 Out of jail (Kajang Prison), 3 Feb, 2000

278 The mention date is 16 Feb, 2000

279 Contempt of court - This is another journey has to go – mention, proceeding and judgement. No doubt this is the lowest court. There is another higher, high court and appeal court.

280 That psychiatric matter

'All situations are likely to be inside out, upside down, more over Illegitimate sexual first then only thinking about married; send to prison first then only find out when the 'mention' and 'proceeding' are'. That is *Jabatan Agama Islam Selangor*[281](JAIS) during UMNO tenancy. That the sound also like JAIS is *Jabatan Agama Islam Sesat*[282]

A lot of outcry from that defendant to JAIS chief director, Selangor 'syariah' court lawyers committee, so many committee and so many places just turn quiet except Bar Council[283] and Karpal Singh and Co. That how the professional is and how to deny? Moreover it was considered 'wrong addresses' and Karpal Singh wrote 'beyond their expertise' and returns all documents it is about fifteen dollars courier charges. No barking, shouting howling or label themselves as Islamic 'jihad' or some sort like that. **'Real Professional'**

There are the role models from Islamic institutions it selves to violence the Islamic rules[284] in the exact and the right place without an embarrassment at all. They really rape their own mothers.

Break-down societies, demoralization of Malay youth today are definitely their full responsibility.

Their criminal was in the sight of God and man.

7.5 - Canning and Cruel

(From story of 5.3.2)

Admonishing is cruel if you think so. But there also cruel to be good – worse like father canning the son for not praying

In Muslim, Prophet Muhammad asks to do so.

---

[281] Islamic Dept. in Selangor

[282] 'Sesat' is sense for mislead.

[283] Malaysia Bar Council – 5 May, 2000; defendant sent the letter with full detail.
With very high professionalism on 8 May, 2000 already on action. The date was fixed to be first day of proceedings (still without mention). Bar Council was come to the court to change of the judge sine die. The judge himself (MOHD NAIM MOKHTAR) acknowledge to defendant in present of plaintive lawyer (MOHD ZAIDI MOHD ZAIN) after had call to the chamber.
Note: Bar Council dated 10 May, 2000 sent a letter (ref; BC/M/4/2000) and forwarded all together with defendant's letter, documents + recorded cassette to the right authority and acknowledge the acceptance of that 'inadvertently' received – suppose not to them.

[284] In the house of Islamic court of justice where the principles must be upheld

At the end there is no father, no canning but the son continuously pray (mean he washes his face, hand & feet 5 time per day – good isn't it?) and this time to the grandchild.

So what do you want to say about admonishing and cruel? Very subjective isn't it?

Is commando training cruel? You have choice to be trained in hotel air-condition room plus chicken chop or roasted chicken as dinner, sleeping bed and hot shower?

Sultan Ahmad Shah.

If we look for Sultanate of Pahang Malaysia, Sultan Ahmad Shah at septuagenarian he be able to jogging every morning as his pilot and aircraft engineer cannot cope with him. Moreover polo, not just horse riding.

His fitness and healthy is just because he 'cruel' to himself.

No pain no gain. He had hundred per cent choices not to do that and just to lay down on lazy chair for full time. But he doesn't.

Tengku Abdullah.

So with his son Tengku Abdullah; in twentieth he drove and race go-kart himself, not as spectator. Lively watch the even, I was in Kajang Selangor. There are a few lanes in town become as racing track. Challenging! That is how the reality is. He chooses to be 'cruel' to himself. He had choice to be selective. He can choose the only conventional track if he want, much more not involve at all in that sports. But he doesn't. One can see his fitness now.

Vladimir Putin

Severe / rough training as army does is good. Why we must worry about admonishing or canning (not killing isn't it?) for education. So with QC in factories is. You want to sell a car (from your factory) of how assembler did become rhombus in shape? Then your wife will be slightly ahead in line of you as driver. With just little bit ahead of you the whole nation she wants to control?

We better close down the factory with that kind of quality of car. HEROT!!²⁸⁵ Brother!

---

²⁸⁵ 'Herot' or 'Erot' it mean distorted

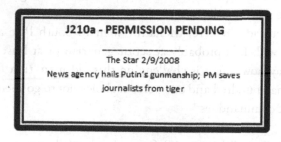

286

What we can say about this?
See all the 'terms';

- Bomber pilot,
- Judo expert,
- Tough-guy image,
- Fitness-mad,
- Bare-chested with fishing rods & rifles
- Then tiger tamer.
- Agile and timely 'sharp' to save journalist from tiger.

He is not ordinary man, 8 years presidency then PM of that such big country

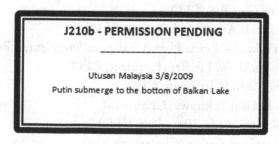

287

This! Real horrible
Just mini submarine, 4 hours, 1.4km deep in the world's deepest lake, Balkan Lake. Observation on his own vision.
Not dreadful enough?

286   News, The Star, Sept 2,2008
287   News, Utusan Malaysia, Aug 3,2009

Yes but he the real 'expensive man', he got choice not to go that expedition and not like some special task commandoes.

I would like to add in here, Mahathir went to South Pole at golden ages definitely on his will. It is probably at septuagenarian or at least sexagenarian. See! All the Malay how much is challenging this old man 'trait (not traitor) of Tun Razak'. He had hundred and one percent choice not to go there, also not like those special task commandoes.

That's right; all of all his (Putin) fitness is not easily come. He must ready and be able to 'cruel' to himself. Then, why we need to worry about canning the son. I used to it and we must listen to any advice if it would become 'compulsory' admonishment to adhere just for our own sake like that QC case. Otherwise; 'HEROTttttt....., man...

7.6 - MSC and California

(From the story of 5.3.1)

MSC is Multimedia Super Corridor– Architectural by Dr. Mahathir.

International Advisory Panel Council was form on 16 January 1997 and first meeting in California, chaired by Dr Mahathir himself.

Most of officers attended were top management i.e. Chairman, President and CEO, like Microsoft is by Bill Gate himself. So with all top companies as;

- IBM – Low Gerstner (CEO)
- Apple – Gilbert Amelio (Chairman, CEO)
- Hewlett Packard – Lewis Platt (Chairman, President, CEO)
- Compaq – Eckhard Pfeiffer (President, CEO)
- Acer – Stan Shih (Chairman, CEO)
- Fujitsu – Tadashi Sekizawa (Chairman)
- Sony – Nobuyuki Idei (President, CEO)
- Motorola – Gary Tooker (Chairman)
- NTT – Naboru Miyawaki (Vice-president, Senior Executive)
- Siemen Corp. – Dr. Heinrich von Pierer (Chairman)
- LG Group – Bon Moo Koo (Chairman)
- Softbank – Masayohi Son (Chairman, CEO)

7.7 - Save Energy and Solar Energy

From footnote in 2.1 – Common Practice

A. By unplug of that phone charger (we save energy) it is contribution to the world which inclusively demanded by Prophet Muhammad and Islam. Personal Heaven tally counter will count up. Wasting is satanic ways and contradiction to authentic Islamic faith.

   i. Malay 'NATO' (No Action Talk Only) will not follow as their point of view just through 'small hole' and 'short-sighted' to their immediate and current interest only.

   ii. What we did practically (on real ground) related to Kyoto Protocol[288]? Just like other typical Malays – for show on everything, take photograph then thick precious documents on table finally in showcase?

   iii. Since then is there any movement like Nokia does? As 'particle count' in Islamic ways we are mutually with non-Muslim take care of our universe. Don't look small for small contribution – just a few cents per message (SMS) it created seventeen million dollars per day in Malaysia in last seven or eight years. Refer next the above (part 2.1 – Common Practice), cost saving with $0.086 per piece land up for $258,000 per year (Taguchi, 1989, p. 138) in that particular industries.

B. That is small thing never happen, how about solar energy? We are among 'wealthiest' and wasted countries. A lot of cronies are going to bath on implementing of solar power? Technologies changes are for the sake of the country as well as universe. Where we are standing?

   i. Listen! The Malay Mail news Mac 8, 1901 reported a lot of bullock-cart and *'perahu'*(manually rowing boat) operators lost their income due to train (rail operating) services between KL and Klang. We must sense and adopt the changes as fast as possible as what our Chinese does.

   ii. Listen!! Their ancient came to Malaya don't know anything about ICT and computer technologies but now they are ahead of everything. Worse we the Malay 'applied handbrake' most of the time in order to keep distance and maintain as not only mules but as lazy mules moreover a lot of talking shit and politicking forever.

---

[288] It is congratulation to Mr Kornelis Blok upon your Peace Noble Price winner as draftsman of Kyoto Protocol.

iii. It is next 3 or 4 year election, now we continuously talking about? When to work? All of arse-lickers / sycophants had no problem as they always feed by someone of '*haram*' money.

iv. Last Mahathir times, today win election tomorrow '*bersih*' (clean) poster and start work – no more politic. Politic is another 5 years. Opposition parties still got chance in survival. Then they had no time to round the clock attacking government. They also must have some work in order to 'silence' them. The government must clever enough.

C. There should be no embattlement with Dr Mahathir. Make use!

i. That was the God gift us we never realise. He only likes buffalo to plough our farm. Then we are blatantly stupid because we ourselves like to be a buffalo to plough the farm.

ii. We not even 0.01% of his. Hasina of Bangladesh really knows and appreciated.

iii. We should study this a few things to justify our stupidity – how MSC is in full detail and look forward to following 7.8 - 'Emma Maersk and Tanjung Pelepas'.

iv. We just imagine how much credit should be to Dr Mahathir. He is the man with never over proud much less shouting like some other Malay leader. He also never summon any his political nemesis, isn't it?

v. I'm talking about the global scope. Let simply hold the globe, where the Emma is then Tanjung Pelepas. Then we imagine how many countries in this world and why should be Malaysia in the line beside how small Malaysia is. If other Malay leaders....... two hundreds over years shouting (if they can live).

D. Before we go to Emma Maersk, I would like to call our attention to think;

a. How much work to change Langkawi to like now?

b. How easy outside world to join us like LIMA (Langkawi International Maritime and Air Show)? They come?

c. Le Tour De Langkawi? (Bicycle racing) International participation? I heard certain party want to sabotage Mahathir? To start that LTDL not from Langkawi?

d. They are not sabotage to Mahathir but for the country to satisfy their satanic will. They want to cheat International participant as they don't know what Langkawi is? What will happen? That mentality they are? Cheating! They think international participants so stupid like our local professional arse-licker?

e. Now they also sabotage whatever Mukriz (Mahathir's son) done on his tenancy as chief minister of Kedah? Real satanic! They should know in civilized society the successor must continue whatever in the predecessor[289] with some adaptation if needed and not sharp cut to back-off?

f. Since fifth PM Abdullah, now the government purchase order cannot be trusted[290]. It can cancel anytime. The government paper can turn to be toilet paper, cannot be hold anymore. Bankers also not trust to government project. Everywhere suspicious. They are king of liar.

g. Those times I heard pariah mentality in India is so great. Everywhere you can see abandoned, partial finish bridges (stop in the middle of the river) and I ask that Indian friend who visited South India, why? When they change in the leader, the projects will abandon. They create new one for them. Corruption is super fantastic.

  i. I just quite listening and the question arouse in my mind, "it can be like that?" as I never see in our country that time.

  ii. Now? We are pariah; grand pariah and king of pariah as in India were civilized.

h. How easy we can participate and become one of venue of the world F1 calendar? How many countries in this world?

  i. We are third world; the country is small and come in later stage. They join in and give us room?

  ii. Before that we must prepare proper circuit (Sepang) isn't it? Or they come with racing cars first and look for the place where can race?

  iii. Is it at par with Silverstone and Albert Park? There you are and where Mahathir is.

i. Don't forget about successful result of 98 CHOGM and there are outcries to look for the Olympic later as confidence can be seen in that event.

j. How easy you can influence to Bill Gate (1997) and all top executives of world leading company in ICT (refer to MSC) to look your face to chairs the meeting at one go? They had time to schedule and solely

---

289 So like businesses. Do we think when take over any business we only take a profit and simply open new books? All other thing simply closed?

290 In Islamic faith, trust and promise very important and it will reflect to whom you are either Muslim or Satan.

assign for you to hear what you want to say? Mahathir does and without braggart or show off since most of our people don't know at all.

k. We cannot varnish what Mahathir does as some actors try to condemn P.Ramlee in order to evoke himself.

    i. For example, one of his movie, 'Ibu Mertua Ku' he made for about two hours show. In fact if you give to Yusuf Haslam the movie can be elongate until 52 weeks. That how compact his works. We suppose not if 5 years' work it is only worth about one day value. Very costly!

Solar;

These two were extracting from my proposal 'Solar Park' (not solar farm as usual). (It is from attachment 04).

Solar park di Sepanyol

This is **my own paper work**; the proposal to so many Malaysia governments' bodies through Najib's parliamentary area.

Most of my paper works (even a few pages of papers) were professionally done. This is my big problems to publisher always accused this is from the book. This is from scratch 100% single handed of mine! My presentation so professional, what to do?

Unfortunately here was photographic of 150 sun carriers to emphasis to government, how difficult in European countries to track the sun – need to omit due to copyright.

Fakta:

* 150 SunCarrier
* Setiap satu seluas 287.5m² (lebih kurang sama dengan 17m x 17m)
* Dia 'track' berubah (align the surface) ikut matahari tiap 10 minit secara automatik.
* Mencukupi untuk lebih 6,100 rumah (4 orang penghuni) dengan purata 3,500kWh setahun (lk 292kWh/bulan = RM63.60 sebulan)
  * o 3,500kWh x RM0.218/kWh (harga TNB) = RM763.00 setahun
  * o Setamaan RM 63.60 sebulan

287.5m² x 150 unit = 43,125m² ← Jumlah permukaan modules (solar panel)
3500kWh/tahun x 6100 rumah = 21,350,000 kWh ← Jumlah kuasa terhasil setahun

Kalau di PAP Tg Batu;

* Katakan solar panel atas bumbung rumah, 60 m² (= 8.5m x 7m) tiap satu.
* Rumah = 200 buah
  * o Maka jumlah keluasan solar panel, 60 m² x 200 rumah = 12,000 m²

43,125m² → 21,350,000kWh setahun (=21.4juta kWh, ...oleh 150 buah panel)
12,000m² → 21,350,000/43,125 x 12,000 = 5,940,870kWh setahun (=6 juta kWh,...oleh 200 rumah)
200 rumah (60 m²) → 5,940,870kWh setahun
Hasil dari sebuah rumah → 5,940,870/200 = 29,704kWh setahun. → 2475kWh/bln = RM539.60/bulan.
**kalau pakai 59.60 sebulan, maka RM 500 boleh dijual kpd TNB sebulan(pd harga bekal oleh TNB)
**Kira-kiranya,... kalau pakai 175kWh sebulan, tuan rumah mendapat lebihan 2300kWh sebulan, yakni 2300 x RM0.15/kWh (katakan harga beli oleh TNB, bukannya RM0.218)= RM345.00 sebulan.

Solar Park

Kalau kualiti dan kecekapan peralatan rendah sedikit dari yang di Sepanyol itu , tuan rumah akan mendapat antara RM200-300 sebulan.

Jadi,....

200 x RM500.00 (harga pakai -TNB) = RM 100,000 sebulan atau RM 1.2juta setahun.

→ PAP menghasilkan (lebih pakai) tenaga letrik dari solar sebanyak RM1.2 juta setahun.

Kita rumuskan semula........

Dari hal Sepanyol

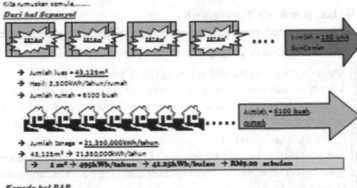

→ Jumlah luas = 43,125m²
→ Hasil: 3,500kWh/tahun/rumah
→ Jumlah rumah = 6100 buah

→ Jumlah tenaga = 21,350,000kWh/tahun
→ 43,125m² = 21,350,000kWh/tahun

| → 1 m² → 495kWh/tahun → 41.25kWh/bulan → RM9.00 sebulan |

Kepada hal PAP

- Katakan 60m² (=8.5m x 7m)/rumah
- Katakan 200 buah rumah terlibat → 12,000m² → 5,940,000kWh/tahun(RM1,294,920.00)

Utk sebuah rumah,

- 60m² x 41.25kWh/bln = 2,475kWh/bln.
- Kalau pakai 175kWh/bln (RM38.15 sebulan), maka ada lebihan 2,300kWh/bln(RM501.40 sebulan) dan boleh boleh balik ke TNB
- Kalau TNB boleh beli balik RM0.15/kWh (TNB jual RM0.218), setiap rumah masih boleh menghasilkan(lebih dari pakai) RM345.00 sebulan (=RM69,000 sebulan oleh 200 rumah = RM828,000 setahun).
- Kalau kecekapan solar panel dan China ini 75% dari di Sepanyol tu, sebuah rumah masih boleh menghasilkan (lebih dari pakai) RM258.75 sebulan (RM51,750 oleh 200 rumah = RM621,000 setahun)

Kita kena buat kajian semula.
Ini hanya berdasarkan satu fakta sahaja.
Bahkan sekarang lebih efisyen.

By: zulpuzeh(019-3358254); 2/7/2013   Page 2 of 2

The first one is 150 sun carriers in Pozohondo, Spain. It track and align the surfaces to the sun every ten minutes. It is enough for 6,100 houses of 4 persons at usages of 3,500kWh per year per house. Total will be 21,350,000kWh per annum.

My concern in proposal was very special place in Datuk Najib's parliamentary area, 200 houses under single management Projek Agropolitan Pekan[291]. It can be systematic and only can do. Otherwise it will be 'colourful' like fanfare and chaotic

To cut it short, I present the calculation and the facts.

200 houses (60m²) will give 5,940,870kWh per year (against Pozohondo efficiency)

Each house will earn about RM539.60/month in value at the price of RM0.218/kWh.

If the price of selling back to the grid is less let say RM0.15 only each house still can get RM345.00/month redundancy after deducting his own use about 175kWh.

After all consideration and calculation in my proposal minus all domestic use that project can earn about RM1.2 million/year[292] redundancy.

With aggressive latest technologies in China and enhancement on equipment now the project will jump up to about two or three million dollars per year at least.

Is this a problem for you Datuk Najib? It is your crony or 'rakyat'?

We must accept changes for the 'rakyat' of 30 million and global green effect rather than two or three crony. Otherwise our fuddy-duddy has to maintain that bullock carts — no train, no car, and no bus between KL-Klang as 1901.

7.8 - Emma Mærsk and Tanjung Pelepas

Everybody was invited to see this documentary;

World's Biggest Ship of 2015 (x20 Titanic) full documentary — Emma Mærsk

In minutes of 00:50 sec; "It's one of the busiest ports on the planet ...." Tanjung Pelepas in Malaysia"

On the minute of (05:00 and 05:40) — there was map from Malaysia to Suez

On 06:01 — Map — it is reveal and the writing of word 'Tanjung Pelepas' straight to Suez

On 43:40 — "Touch the dock, get in schedule, 14 days, 13,000km, ...to Malaysia"

---

[291]   This is housing park for solely participants of Felda project of palm oil for that particular area. Their skim is they like a worker to the management right now until certain period. Then become theirs when maturity. It means now in one control. That why I can propose for synchronise and systematic mean.

[292]   Base on efficiency at Pozohondo. In fact here will be much more efficiency and now the enhancement of equipment will make up many fold better.

See what the proud? International documentary! Big portion of that documentary is about relation with Tanjung Pelepas.

Selected Tanjung Pelepas is one of not many ports for Emma Mærsk.

293

294,

295.

Just see how exceptional infrastructure done by Mahathir to cater that kind of big ship. Then it is how many of that kind in this world?

Consecutively back-up support by proper highway network to complete as Second Link highway.

---

293   ZP's, Jan 2009, one of ordinary size containers vessel approaching Port of Tanjung Pelepas

294   ZP's, Jan 2009, Tanjung Pelepas

295   ZP's, Jan 2009, Tanjung Pelepas.

We just imagine how much ingenious and the work for so great infrastructure for that remarkable point in the world map. Then you acquired that special privilege throughout the world – world recognition.

Let learn (in-house) that is a clever man. He not is doing the entire thing. Then we see the result? We suppose to learn and close to him – our 'junk' asset. His 22 years proven still we cannot see?. Let see what Saidina Ali[296] said; "A clever man not only can differentiate between good and bad, moreover he can extract of the goodness within two bad things. Try! Try to take any good thing because everything was real existed in this country earlier – not hallucination and perfection of fairy tale kingdom.

I think he not conquer everything. All 'buffaloes with adequate grass' work for him. Not like Abdullah, all the grass he wants to wipe out. Then it horning him. Then he knows how stupid he is. Suppose KFC, pizza or burger just enough for the boss, not all the grass together.

7.9 - Hina Hakim Syaitan

J250a - PERMISSION PENDING
_____
Harian Metro 2/2/2000
The contempt of 'Satanic Judge'. The journalist wrote distinctly with 95% truth of every step monitoring which is much more credited to defendant....

J250b - PERMISSION PENDING
_____
Harian Metro 2/2/2000
The contempt of 'Satanic Judge'.
Continuing page....and worse it is reflect to their stupidity

---

[296] The fourth caliph in Muslim

7.10 - Religious

Religious resolves the entire problem

- Drug addiction
- Smuggling
- Road safety and accident
- Corruption and misconduct
- Loyalty to the ruler
- Unmarketable Y generation in occupation
- Immoral
- Wickedness
- ..
- ..
- ..
- Up to stop smoking still bound under religious problem solving

This is the perfect way, 100% guaranteed success and at zero cost.

The guy who teaches me was non-Muslim Chinese.

For me, he is very sincere till now I already stop smoking for about 33 years.

Thanks to the God by sending me to him.

This is not a business!

This is not a campaign for stop smoking.

Just an option of help to anybody who is willing to stop

Confirmed, proven and most effective, 100%

Cost is RM0.00 as curative power was inside of each smoker. Not necessary to hunting around to find anywhere.

Now please forward to '16 years stop smoking' and comeback here again.

Finish (the 'stop smoking')? Is it great?

That is how religious works. It is 'inside' some sort like your computer's processor – 'Intel inside'.

I would like to call a little attention to think.

The question - What should I take to reduce my weight now? It is obese

The answer - 'fasting'

Comment – Most of people take wrong action. How far you go around not for the actual solution it won't solve the problem. My friend of mind had spent out a few thousand for slimming session. He adhere all it works. After that it back again as he back to his earlier habit. So the actual solution never runs off.

7.10.1 - 16 YEARS STOP SMOKING AND ABOUT ADMONISHING

As I said the guy who teach me was non-Muslim Chinese

Those days I smoke for seven years

Since 1982 I tried stop smoking. First time I success for about 3 months. Then I did about 6 months. After that I tried again.

The formula of my practising is to reduce the number of cigarette and go to 'mild' type. Then I smoke mild Peter Stuyvesant.

I always buy from nearest shop next to my house in Southern Park in Klang. If I not mistaken it was *'Lintang Tamarind'*.

One day after I bought a cigarette, the shop owner[297] stops me and asks

"Why you buy this cigarette? Last time Dunhill. You want to stop smoking?"

His Malay language is literate. The way he acts is like to admonish small boy

I admitted (to stop smoking).

"If you want to stop smoking, simply follow my 'divine guidance' (advice). I had already 16 years stop smoking. No touch at all". He had practised and advice.

"This 'divine guidance' is very easy, stopped! Don't smoke at all even a stick, *'haram terus'*[298]. That all you need"

He stops for a while. "Do you understand?"

The only my eyes flicker, not even admitted or nod

Consecutively he continues his 'preaching' as I am turning muted.

"You are Muslim! Last fasting month you always buy in small packet (7 sticks). It is meaning you are fasting. You are being able to not smoking because you are fasting, and because of your religious. That mean you had strength (strong will). That what you should! (use it)

You simply choose one special good day, decided and totally stop! Don't touch even a stick. If you gradually reduce, it doesn't works! Falsehood! After that you will be back again. Don't trust any medicine. The medicine is your heart of yourself.

You want to stop, stopped! Otherwise no need to stop. That's all. You also not will be rich by stop smoking".

---

[297] It is Sexagenarian or septuagenarian. I am still clearly seeing his face talking. His face and style look alike late Sultan Sallehuddin Abdul Aziz Shah, the King of Selangor.

[298] Totally forbidden

His 'preaching' really exceptional and stick in my mind[299].

It is about a time I am waiting for my first baby. Then I make up my mind and decided to choose as the baby born I will stop smoking. It was Aug 10, 1983.

Thanks to the God of my success (up to now) my trial series of 3 months, 6 months and now the longest about 33 years.

Feel healthy. Last time every month I need to see doctor for fever, caught and flu. There were a few times I had experience on chest pain. It is real painful like to explode or die. I am feeling promise not to smokes again after recover.

It is never happen. The addiction is too high overwriting everything.

That Chinese 'divine guidance' is right. Religious and your heart are heightened by Prophet Muhammad. 13 years on initial of his task was about heightening of behavioural

"I was touched by his kindness and sincerity. By then with his guidance 'I no more buy any cigarette'[300] from his shop. He is also on risk if I get mad – this is admonishing.

There got killing case just because admonishing.

After exceeding 20 years stop smoking, I still feel (mild) like to smoke back again. There how severe the addiction is. Not to play a foul. But now is no more.

A long the way of those 20 years the only thing works is 'Islamic hearted feeling to resist'.

Thanks to the non-Muslim Chinese old man. You are the great man.

If smoke addiction is like that we just imagine the involvement in drug addiction. It is most probably 'total losses' for the most cases – no cure.

The only thing had is religious and heart. It is easy just a few words.

'The good things never come cheap'[301]

'Soft to say but hard to adopt[302]'

---

[299] Admonishing by non-Muslim to Muslim to utilise what they had (Islamic faith) for the good of universe – Real noble-dead by nobleman – preciously heart and mind.

[300] 'I no more buy any cigarette' - preciously heart and mind is beyond religious, racial and business.

[301] 'The good things never come cheap' - BMW motto midst of 80iest.

[302] Consecutively Prophet Muhammad relay his 'key message' against this matter in the last sermon. "I leave you with two things to uphold. You will never misled, it is Quran and 'Hadith' (all about his words, speech, preaches, character and behaviour)" – so where the Muslim is? All over the practises are deviated to satanic will? Simply kill here and there for the most of 'forbidden blood' blatantly uphold with bull power without brain and against Prophet Muhammad?

7.10.2 - JACKO

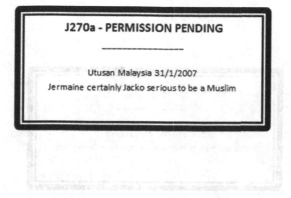

J270a - PERMISSION PENDING

Utusan Malaysia 31/1/2007
Jermaine certainly Jacko serious to be a Muslim

303

Let see non popular case

Jermaine confidence Jacko seriously to be a Muslim

"......I want he leave America and stay in the peaceful place where the peoples pray five time per day"

We set other thing aside we only talking about the fact it is religious and problem solving

The man needed a religious, that it.

The problem now is like what happening to Malay in Malaysia. The first man like drunk

---

303 News; Utusan Malaysia, Jan 31,2007

7.10.3 - BRITAIN AND JOHN MAJOR

J270b - PERMISSION PENDING

———————

Berita Harian 28/12/1993
Britain obligate to the religious subject – John Major

[304]

John Major wants Britain to obligate religious subject such as Islam, Christian, Hindu, Buddhist, Sikh, and Jewish. It should start as early as five years
There has certain reasons but the main issue is as what we discuss.

———————

[304]   News; Berita Harian, Dec 28, 1993

7.10.4 - MARILYN MONROE

```
┌─────────────────────────────────┐
│  J270c - PERMISSION PENDING     │
│  _____            │
│                                 │
│  Utusan Malaysia 13/9/1987      │
│  Marilyn 'still continuing in alive'; photo & article │
└─────────────────────────────────┘
```

```
┌─────────────────────────────────┐
│  J270d - PERMISSION PENDING     │
│  - - - - - - - - - - - -        │
│                                 │
│  Utusan Malaysia 13/9/1987      │
│  Continuing page ....Marilyn 'live as legend' │
└─────────────────────────────────┘
```

305

Let see Marilynn Monroe and her problem

{Over writing time (1987) it is about 25 years upon her deceased}

If we properly observe the main problem is only around 'religious' matter.

Her life is full of pressure and she has to endure suffering in searching true loving life

> …………Hollywood is the places where the people are prepare to pay one thousand dollars for a kiss and fifty cents for your soul.
>
> …………fantasy world of Hollywood – end up ruin of that.

---

305 News; Utusan Malaysia, Sept 13, 1987

......Marilyn try to overcome pressure on her mental sickness and needed psychiatric the entire life.

.... At the ages of 36 she had committed suicide in Los Angeles on August 4, 1962

That is how Marilyn Monroe (Norma Jean) is.

Then appreciating not simply vanishes, emerging of 'Marilyn Skirt' in Chicago but for what?

----- end -----

It is rare unknown author emerge from **low class society try to voice out their problem and suggestion.** This, the one!

He believe whoever experienced as real commando only know and could talk as real commando, otherwise just like white paper to write and sketch from outside sources

About the Book

The front cover shows the boy call the girl and pointed down 'where the outcast is' – the beach of Nenasi, Pekan, Pahang.

Everybody can simply or serious read. This is the prediction by 'Nujum Pak Belalang'** and definitely happen in short time unless 'something happen' now.

Clear track was created for all Malay to 'Cassandra Crossing' and fully astride welcome to Chinese. They only need to repeat it on bigger scale as Lee Kuan Yew shows how to take over Singapore. If it is coolness, comfort, very peaceful and 'gentleman handover' like Dr Mahathir hand over to Abdullah Badawi, why not? Then everybody can live efficiently under Chinese like Singapore.

Right now Chinese had started their 'responsibility' in Penang to take over. Congratulation! Malaysian Chinese is about 100 time clever than world's cleverest (Jews). They are like 'sun' and Jews just like 'wind' to open the shepherd's shirt.

Be relax, the world will be end soon.

**Malay folklore; Nujum is Astrologer, Pak Belalang (name). He is not genuine astrologer. All his tasks come from real information from his son. He just pretends to 'observe' in his clay pot like monitor/screen.

December 2016.

Printed in the United States
By Bookmasters